2/14/07

Barbara,

Enjoy!

Mary Bigler

Mary Bigler's Lessons Learned

Mary Bigler's Lessons Learned

Teaching and Speaking

Mary Bigler

Reading Success Center
Ann Arbor, Michigan

Printed in the United States of America.

FIRST EDITION

Library of Congress Registration Number
available upon request

Library of Congress Cataloging-in-Publication Data
available upon request

ISBN 0-9770316-0-8

Reading Success Center
1225 Fairmount Drive
Ann Arbor, MI 48105-2831

Cover design and text format by Sans Serif, Inc.
Cover photo by Andy Oberdick

For my teachers: *family*

friends

teachers

students

parents

colleagues

audiences

Without them there would be no stories to tell.

For all teachers everywhere entrusted with our future—the children of today

Contents

Contents

Contents

Thank You,
Family and Friends

Mother, Maxine, and Father, Ernie: for a happy childhood, for exemplary role models, for making this all possible

Husband, Bill: for providing me with the freedom to pursue the life that resulted in these stories, for making me believe that I could write this book, for countless hours of editing, for sparing me from the business details involved in completing this task, for our forty fun-filled years together

Daughter, Beth: for assuring me that teachers needed to hear my stories, for being my sounding board and cheerleading me through this project, for editing, for being a wonderful daughter, for my future

Brother, Jim: for hours upon hours of painstaking proofreading and grammar and usage corrections, for creativity, for always being ready to come to my aid

The rest of my family: for reading my book, for offering helpful suggestions and loving support, for photo rating, for computer support, for being such great family

Friend, Joyce: for thorough and thoughtful proofreading under pressing time constraints, for being a model of how to live life to its fullest, for being my teaching soul mate

Forethoughts

I was born to be a teacher. At least, that's what my mother claimed and mothers are usually right, aren't they? Mom said that I began at age seven when I gathered my younger siblings and neighbor kids and tried teaching them the alphabet and how to count. Now, after forty years in the classroom, I still love every day that I go to work. I cannot imagine not teaching. Teaching is more than my job. It is my life.

I have many stories to share, as all teachers do. It will not be possible to continue to share them in my classroom and in presentations around the world forever. I have set them down here in the hope that others will enjoy and perhaps benefit from them.

For years I have resisted writing these stories because I did not want to invade people's privacy. I have finally decided that these stories are too good not to pass on. With privacy in mind, I have worked hard to keep secret the identity of the students, parents, staff and audience members, schools and businesses found in these accounts. Often I have used only first names. On some occasions I have included last names. Last names are all fictitious with the exception of those listed below. Those who lived these stories with me will recognize themselves and their classmates, but that is unavoidable. While the names are fictitious, I assure you that every story is true.

I do use the real names of some people. These people are my husband, colleagues, a teacher, and a neighbor of mine, whose names I want you to know and people who, I am sure, would not object. The real names that I have used are Beanie Stein (my Iowa neighbor), Miss Boddicker, Joe G. Boddicker, Bob Tomsich, Nancy Johnson, Leland Jacobs and my husband, Bill Bigler.

I have chosen to tell stories that are interesting, educational, amusing, uplifting or inspiring. I have deliberately decided not to tell stories that cast people or schools in a bad light. I will leave that for others. We already have many more critics than we need. I do include a few negative stories but only when positive messages flow from them.

I have divided the stories into three sections. The first section includes stories that occurred while I was teaching as well two stories about teachers of mine and one story about a teacher of my husband's **(Teaching)**. The second section features one lesson learned from my father and one from my mother **(Dad and Mom)**. The third section contains stories that happened or that I heard while speaking at conferences and in-service meetings throughout the world **(Speaking)**.

While I address my stories to teachers, I believe that anyone who cares about raising and educating young people will find value and inspiration in the following pages. I have had many remarkable experiences in my years of learning, teaching and speaking. I hope you find these lessons that I have learned enjoyable, helpful and memorable.

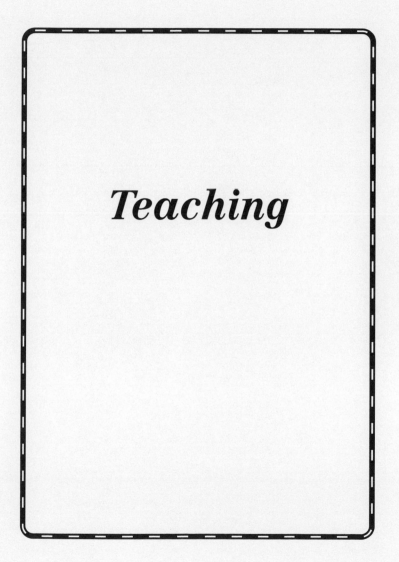

Teaching

M y teaching career began in 1965. I started as a high school history teacher and then moved to the middle level as a history and English teacher. Following librarian John Cotton Dana's dictum, "Who dares to teach must never cease to learn," I earned an M.A. in History along the way. Having so many students at the secondary level who struggled with reading, I decided to acquire elementary certification so I could work where so much of reading instruction occurs. Then I obtained an M.A. in Reading. I eventually became a reading consultant and diagnostician, earned my doctorate at the University of Michigan and joined the faculty of Eastern Michigan University where I am presently involved with preparing current and future teachers to teach students to read and write.

All but three of the following stories are about people that I have known and experiences that I have had teaching during the last forty years.

Three stories are about other teachers. I tell one story of an extraordinary teacher who impressed upon me a great lesson when I was a child. I relate an instructive albeit painful lesson that I learned from a different teacher as a teenager. I share one story that is not my own. It happened to my husband, Bill. I am telling it because it is the best example of the power of positive teaching that I have encountered. I learned of Bill's life-altering experience before I began teaching. It has influenced my way of relating to students ever since.

I touch the future.
I teach.

Christa McAuliffe

Miss Boddicker

The historian Henry Adams said, "Teachers affect eternity. They do not know where their influence ends." I think of that almost every time I walk into a classroom. I also think of Miss Boddicker.

I grew up in rural Iowa. Miss Boddicker was my fifth grade teacher. She had recovered from polio at a time when many people did not. She walked with a pronounced limp and her hands were rigid. She was the best teacher that I ever had.

One bitter cold day in the middle of January we were working on a science project in our classroom when one of the kids complained, "I can't do this."

7

Miss Boddicker said, "I want all of you to go get your coats and hats. We're going outdoors. Roger, get some small pieces of scrap paper and pencils and bring them with you."

We bundled up and got ready to go outside. We knew that it wasn't time for recess but, when Miss Boddicker said to do something, you did it and you didn't ask why.

She went to the closet and wrangled the shovel out. Since her hands were rigid, it was quite a struggle.

One of the boys offered to help her with it.

She said, "Thank you, but I can do it myself."

We walked down the steps. Miss Boddicker had difficulty because she had to hold on to the banister with one hand and lug the shovel with the other.

One of the girls offered to help her.

She repeated, "Thank you, but I can do it myself."

We went out to the schoolyard.

Miss Boddicker told us to go stand underneath

Joe G. Boddicker's tree. We only had one tree in our schoolyard. Joe G. Boddicker was Miss Boddicker's uncle. He had donated the land for the school many years before so we always called the tree, "Joe G. Boddicker's tree."

It must have been ten degrees below zero that day. The ground was frozen solid. Miss Boddicker proceeded to try to dig a hole. Remember, she was lame in one leg and could not grasp the shovel for leverage, so it was an arduous undertaking.

Several boys offered to help her, but she refused all offers of assistance. While we froze, she managed to make a small indentation in the ground. Then she turned to us and said, "I want each of you to take a piece of scrap paper and write the word 'can't' on it."

We did as we were told.

Then she instructed, "Now, I want each of you to come over here and put your piece of paper in this hole."

One by one we ceremoniously dropped our papers in the hole.

She turned the shovel on its side, covered the hole with the black dirt and snow and patted it down.

Then she turned to us and said, "I don't ever want to hear the word 'can't' again. There is no such thing as 'can't.' We have buried 'can't' under Joe G. Boddicker's tree!"

I don't need to tell you that there were thirteen kids in that class who never said "can't" again.

Miss Boddicker lives on in my classroom because, whenever children say that they can't do something, I say, "There's no such thing as 'can't'. I buried 'can't' under Joe G. Boddicker's tree."

Then I tell them the story.

Rodney's Field Trip

To all you teachers out there who take children on field trips—I salute you. Polish your halos. You are going to the Good Place. I'm not. I hate field trips. Yes, you're right. They are good for the children, so you keep taking them. But, *moi,* I have gone on my last field trip. Let me tell you about an eye-opening lesson that I learned on a field trip.

I got on the bus with the children and noticed that third-grader Rodney had his eyes closed. I don't just mean closed. They were "squintin' shut." I did what most of you would do. I ignored it. You know, if you ignore many things, they go away.

Fifteen minutes into the field trip, Rodney had not opened his eyes.

I looked over and said, "Rodney, do you have a headache today?"

"No," he growled back.

Forty-five minutes into the field trip, Rodney had not opened his eyes. I mean, I've got my eagle eye on the kid and he had not opened his eyes.

So I said, "Rodney, are you having sinus or allergy problems today?"

"No!" he snarled.

One hour and fifteen minutes after we left school, we arrived at the dairy farm. I was at the front of the bus doing "the don'ts." You know, "the don'ts": don't talk to anybody, don't touch anything, don't go to the bathroom without your buddy . . . Don't. *Don't*. DON'T! (I always say that I don't know why we take kids on field trips. We don't let them do one darn thing after we get them there!)

Anyway, Rodney had still not opened his eyes so I looked at him and said, "Rodney, we are getting off the bus now and I would appreciate it if you would open your eyes because I don't want you to step in any cow pies. By the way, just why have you had your eyes closed ever since we left school?"

With that, he snapped open his eyes and said, "Because I don't want to see nothin' on this stupid field trip because I don't want to write about it when we get back!"

Man, Rodney was way ahead of me. It was so true. Every time that we went on a field trip, we would come back and do an experience story.

"Rodney, what did you see on the field trip?" I would pose.

Rodney was showing me. He wasn't seeing "nothin' " on this field trip!

The sacred Jewish text, the Talmud, says, "Much I have learned from my teachers, more from my colleagues, but most from my students."

Tom

My students and I are fellow travelers on an exciting journey. Some days I am the tour guide. Other days they are. Tom led me down a very enlightening and inspiring road.

One year, early in my career, there was a well-mannered, conscientious eleventh-grader in my second-hour American History class. Tom was attentive, asked and answered questions and eagerly participated in class activities.

All was well until the first test. Tom only scored fourteen percent!

I could not believe it. He hardly attempted to answer the essay questions, missed all the matching questions and only got a few of the true/false questions right.

I wrote, "See me after school" at the top of his paper.

He never showed. I was surprised because he seemed so responsible.

The next day, I said, "Tom, where were you yesterday?"

He said, "What do you mean?"

"You were supposed to come in and see me after school."

"I was?"

"Yes. I wrote that on the top of your test."

"Oh. Well, do you want me to come in today?"

"Yes, I do."

He arrived immediately after the last period.

I said, "Tom, what happened on your test?"

He looked down at the floor but didn't say anything.

"Were you sick?"

No response.

"I can't understand how you did so poorly. I know you knew two of the answers because you talked about them in class when we reviewed, so I know you should have gotten those right."

No response.

"Tom, I'm waiting for an explanation."

In a barely audible voice, he mumbled, "I can't read."

I said, "What?"

"I can't read," he said a little more loudly.

"Of course you can read, Tom. I'm serious now. What happened on this test?"

More emphatically, he said, "Mrs. Bigler, I can't read."

No one ever told me that I would have high school students who could not read the textbook or tests. Today, we know that we have many high school students with reading problems, but I am here to tell you that no one ever mentioned that in my teacher education courses in the early 60's. I never knew that it was possible to be in the eleventh grade and not be able to read. So I said, "Read the third true/false statement." I knew that it was an answer that he knew.

Struggling, he read, "Before the vo . . . age [voyage] of Co . . . lum . . . bus [Columbus], E . . . ro . . . pins [Europeans] did not know the Westn [Western] Hem . . . pe . . . here [Hemisphere] ex-ited [existed]."

I was shocked. Tom was haltingly saying some words, mispronouncing others and failing to say some altogether. He was not fluent. He surely could not be understanding what he read. He really couldn't read!

I knew that he was a good listener and that he had learned a great deal from the class lectures, so I started reading the test questions to him.

He could answer them.

I ended up reading the whole test to him and grading him on his verbal responses. He received an eighty-six percent.

I was dumbfounded, but I entered the eighty-six percent in my grade book.

"How do you do in your other classes?"

"To tell the truth, I flunk everything."

"Come on," I said. "What kind of grades do you get?" I am a *very* slow learner.

"Mrs. Bigler, I usually get F's but sometimes teachers pass me because I try and I behave, so I have a few D's."

"What are your best subjects?"

"Drafting and Woodworking."

"So, do you flunk Drafting and Woodworking?"

"Yeah, but I'm good at them."

"How can you be good at them and be flunking?"

"Well, I know how to do the assignments if someone tells me what I am supposed to do. You know, I designed the homecoming float last year and I helped Coach design the cabinets in the locker room and . . . "

I could hardly wait to visit the Drafting/Woodworking teacher and tell him of my discovery.

As soon as Tom was out the door, I hurried to the Drafting teacher's room.

"I just made the most amazing discovery! You know Tom? He can't read. I mean, he really can't read. He got fourteen percent on his history test but, when I read the questions to him and he answered them verbally, he got an eighty-six percent. He knows the history content. He just can't read the test questions. I am going to read his tests to him from now on.

He tells me that he is good in Drafting but gets F's because he can't read the tests and the directions. If someone tells him what he needs to do, he can do it. So, I was thinking, maybe you could read his tests or the directions for projects to him and he would get much better grades."

That veteran teacher gave me a look that said, "Are you nuts?"

He said, "I don't make exceptions nor do I accept excuses. If he can't read the test, he flunks."

"But, if he knows what you are teaching, then he shouldn't be penalized because he can't read," I protested. "You shouldn't be grading him on his reading ability. You should be grading him on his drafting ability."

"Mary, I don't tell you how to teach. Don't you come down here and tell me how to teach."

I was amazed for the second time that afternoon. I thought that I was revealing such an important discovery about Tom that it would surely impact on all his teachers. I found that few were willing to accommodate his problem.

I did succeed in getting his English teacher to make some accommodations for a while, but that eventually fell by the wayside.

I told Tom that he could come after school on the days that we had tests and quizzes and I would read the tests to him. I promised to find someone who would tape the chapters for him (the speech teacher offered that for extra credit to speech students) so Tom could listen to the text and learn about American History.

He ended up getting B's both semesters while flunking every other class that he took.

Tom and I worked out the same arrangement for his senior year for American Government. He received a B+ for the first semester and an A for the second semester.

About two months before graduation (Tom was

not graduating but was being given a certificate of attendance), he appeared at my door after school one afternoon.

"Mrs. Bigler, I was wondering if you would be willing to write a letter of recommendation for me?"

Since I had been writing numerous letters of recommendation for college applications for my seniors, my first thought was, "Oh, no. Surely, Tom doesn't think that he's applying to college, does he?"

So I asked, "What is it that you have in mind in terms of a recommendation?"

"Well," he said, "there's an opening in the City Surveyor's office and I've got it figured out. Surveyors generally work in teams and, as long as I am with someone who can read, I know I can do the work. But I need a letter of recommendation. I did do well in your classes so I was hoping you could write a letter for me."

I was so impressed that, although the system had been telling this kid that he was a failure for years, he had enough confidence to say, "I know I can do the work." I knew in my heart that Tom was going to make it.

I said, "I would be happy to write a letter for you. I can talk about all your character strengths—your honesty, dependability, persistence, creativity and confidence. Now, I have to talk about your reading problem because that is only being fair to any future employer, but I will write a strong letter because I know that you will do your best in whatever you undertake."

I wrote the letter.

In the middle of the summer I received a call, at home, from Tom. "I got the job, Mrs. Bigler. They hired me. I'm going to work in the Surveyor's office. It's just an entry level job, but I'll work my way up."

I had no doubts—until March of the following year. While I was teaching, the principal appeared at my door and said, "Mrs. Bigler, there's a phone call for you in the office. It's someone from the City Surveyor's office. They want to speak with you. I'll watch your class for you while you take the call."

It was with a heavy heart that I walked to the office. I thought, "Oh, no. Something's happened. It must be bad. Why would they call me? Has Tom placed a fire hydrant over a gas main?"

I picked up the phone.

A voice said, "Mrs. Bigler?"

"Yes?"

"This is Mel Grissom, the City Surveyor. I just want to tell you, if you have any other boys at that school that can't read, send them down here. This Tom is the best damn worker I've ever had!"

As the English writer Arnold Bennett says, "Everyone teaches, everyone learns." Tom taught me that, if you have confidence in yourself, you can be successful.

Grammar

When we are faced with curricula that students perceive to be boring, unimportant or repetitious, we need to be creative, daring and dramatic. Sometimes, it helps to be, as the kids would say, "a little weird."

I was assigned to a new building to teach ninth grade English. The principal told me that I was expected to teach grammar for the first nine weeks. I asked if I could teach literature first and work my way into the grammar because I knew grammar was not a popular subject with ninth-graders. I was told that I had to follow the curriculum guide, so grammar it was! I was not worried because I knew a good way to make parts of speech come alive.

So, first period I walked into class and crawled under the desk.

There was an immediate "buzz" with students saying, "What is she doing?" "Is that our teacher?"

I waited for a lull in the noise level and I yelled out, "Where is Mrs. Bigler?"

There was dead silence.

I waited.

No one said anything.

I thought to myself, "Okay, Mary, now you are under the desk and no one is responding. What do you do now?"

When you don't know what else to do, you just continue to do what you have been doing. I called out again, "Where is Mrs. Bigler?"

Finally, one boy in the back of the room, in utter disgust, responded, "Under the desk."

I jumped out and said, " 'Under' is a preposition. Prepositions show relationships between objects. I was *under* the desk."

Then I climbed on top of the desk and said, "Now where is Mrs. Bigler?"

"On the desk," two students reluctantly responded.

" 'On' is a preposition. I was *on* the desk."

There was lots of murmuring. I overheard, "Who else is teaching English first hour?" "Jasmine, who's our counselor? We gotta get out of this class!"

Undeterred, I ran over and stood between two desks and said, "Now where is Mrs. Bigler?"

"Between the desks," replied three students.

I ran around the room for ten minutes demonstrating every preposition I knew. Then I said, "We're going to have a test."

There was a collective gasp and I said, "Oh, don't worry. This is not a paper and pencil test. You're not going to get a grade. I'm going to play a tape. It features a singer who was popular a long time ago. His name is Glen Campbell and he's singing a song called "Gentle on My Mind."

One boy said, "That's stale, lady."

"Hey," I responded, "I'm not playing this song to update your country music knowledge. I'm playing it because it has around thirty-six prepositional phrases."

"Now here's what I want you to do. Whenever you hear a prepositional phrase, I want you to raise your right hand. If you don't know what a prepositional phrase is, just look at your neighbors. When they raise their hands, you raise yours. I won't know if you know what a prepositional phrase is or not. Let's go!"

I turned the tape on. After a few moments of hesitation, they began to thrust their arms in the air with gusto.

When the tape was done, I said, "Tomorrow we're doing nouns."

That morning my ninth-graders did not walk out of class saying, "Geez, we've got to do

boring old parts of speech that we've done five times before." Rather, they walked out saying, "Tomorrow we're doing nouns!" with a degree of engagement and excitement that warmed my heart.

Mr. R

Teachers often say, "What's taught is not what's caught." On this day I felt caught but not taught. If wisdom comes through suffering, then Mr. R made me wise.

My family moved from rural Iowa to urban Michigan over Thanksgiving vacation during my sophomore year of high school. I hated it. I had left all my friends in a small school where everyone had known my family and where I had been popular and respected. I now found myself in a large school where I was unknown and ignored.

It was my first day at the new high school. I was abysmally unhappy. I missed my friends at my old school, thought everyone was staring at me and felt completely out of place. In this wretched state, I entered my sophomore English class as inconspicuously as possible and took an open seat at the back of the room.

Each student was assigned to read a sentence aloud and supply the correct verb. We were taking turns reading the sentences. We were going up and down the rows.

It was fast approaching the time when I would have to read. I dreaded having to read out loud. I did not want to call even the slightest attention to myself. I braced for my sentence. Then it was my turn!

"We were told to wash our hands," I read.

There were several giggles. I didn't know why the kids were laughing. I knew that I had the right verb. I thought the kids were laughing at me because I was new.

Mr. R, the teacher, with all the sensitivity of a thumbtack, said, "Read that again."

I couldn't believe that he had asked me to read it again. I was so embarrassed! I knew that I had the right verb so I read it again exactly as I had read it the first time.

More laughter.

"How do you say the fifth word?" he asked.

"Warsh," I replied.

My classmates laughed.

"Where is the 'r' in that word?" he asked.

"There isn't one," I answered.

"Then why are you putting one there?"

"I don't know. That's the way I say it."

"Where do you come from that they teach you to put 'r's' in words where there aren't any?"

Some kids started going "rrrrrrrrrrrr."

I was mortified as only a fifteen-year-old girl can be. I hated Mr. R. He had embarrassed me in front of my peers on my first day at this stupid, new school.

The memory of that experience is still painful for me today. However, it taught me an important lesson that I have tried to use throughout my teaching career. Treat every student with dignity and respect.

I made my fair share of mistakes as a new teacher so I don't want to judge Mr. R too harshly. He was an inexperienced teacher. I am sure that he learned to handle dialect differences much better as he gained experience and sensitivity.

He should have used this occasion to celebrate our rich and diverse language. He could have said, "What I find so interesting and exciting about our beautiful English language is that we have fascinating variations in how we say things. If we lived in New England, we might put 'r's' at the end of words like 'Americer' and 'idear' or we might drop the 'r' sound as in 'pock' (park) your 'cah' (car). Now we have a classmate who inserts an 'r' sound in the middle of a word. Isn't that interesting?"

He could have taken this opportunity to show that every area of our country, including our own, has distinctive ways of speaking. He could have said, "We Michiganders have our own unique pronunciations, you know."

He might have written the word, "Michigan," on the board.

Then, he might have said, "Let me see the hands of those born and raised in this state. Okay. Would one of you natives say this word for me?"

Chances are good that Michiganders would say "Michigin" instead of "Michigan." He could have shown the class this unique Michigan pronunciation and invited them to search for more. (For "creek," we say "crick." For "roof," we say a double "o" sound that is the same as that in "book." There are many more examples to be found when you start listening for them.)

Instead of making me feel bad about where I came from and how I talked, he could have made me feel special—that I had something unique to contribute to the group. He could have said, "Mary, could you please find out if this pronunciation comes from your previous home or from your mom's home or your dad's home? While Mary is researching this for us, let's all try to find something interesting or unique about each of our families' speech. Bring something in tomorrow to share."

This could have been a great opportunity to make a new student feel special and to enlighten and excite the students about the wonderful richness of our English language. This story reminds us of how important it is to respect all of our students as we work to transform their lives.

The Court House Field Trip

I have a sign in my classroom that says, "Learn from the mistakes of others because you are not going to live long enough to make them all yourself." I wish I had learned about field trips from someone else's mistakes.

After finishing a unit on the judicial system in the first American Government classes that I taught, I decided that I had to take my classes to see a courtroom in action. What better way was there to learn about the legal system than to sit through a trial?

I called the local court case manager to see which cases of interest to high school seniors were on the docket in the next few weeks.

He said there was a divorce case beginning the next week.

I thought, "Well, that might be good. Many of my students would be getting married within a few years. It would be instructive to let them see what happens when it doesn't work out."

It was a great deal of work to arrange for busses to take the kids to the courthouse ten miles away, obtain permission slips from the parents, alert the other teachers to the fact that the students would miss their classes that day and make arrangements for someone to pick the kids up if we were not back in time for them to take the busses home. However, the students' enthusiasm buoyed my spirits and I proceeded full steam ahead.

On the day of the field trip, I boarded the bus with sixty-six seniors and two chaperones.

We arrived at the courthouse, filed into the bench seats and waited.

The bailiff appeared, announced that there were students in the courtroom to observe the trial, warned us not to be disruptive and then announced, "This is the case of Sidney vs. Sidney."

A number of students gasped.

I looked down the row trying to discover what was wrong. I nudged the student next to me and said, "What is it?"

She said, "That's Bob's sister and brother-in-law."

Two rows ahead of where I was seated, I could see Bob, the quarterback of our football team, shift uncomfortably in his seat.

Unaware that Mrs. Sidney's brother's high school government class was in the audience, the Sidneys moved to the plaintiff and defendant's chairs at the front of the courtroom.

Now these were the days before no-fault divorce, so there had to be grounds for the divorce. This meant that there had to be convincing evidence that the marriage could not be saved before it could be dissolved. Consequently, one of the parties had to prove that the other party had done something so serious that the marriage could not be salvaged.

The lawyer for Bob's sister established that the grounds for the divorce were mental cruelty.

As the trial progressed, more and more lurid details of the husband's exploits were being revealed.

I was getting frantic. We had been warned that we were not allowed to leave the trial once it had begun. I was praying, "Dear God, please get us out of here."

While Bob's sister was testifying, her lawyer asked her what her husband had said that had been the "ultimate humiliation."

She said, "I don't think I should say it out loud if there are students in the courtroom."

The judge said, "I order the teacher to remove her students from the courtroom."

There is a God!

I hustled those kids out of there so fast! We boarded the bus and went directly back to school.

We were supposed to have been gone the

whole day, but we were back to school in about an hour and a half. The principal said, "Why are you back?"

I said, "Don't ask."

Court House Field Trip, the Sequel

**I vowed never to take the kids to court again.
That lasted until the next year.**

After we finished our study of the judicial system that following year, the students asked, "Why can't we go to court? Last year's class did."

I was pretty sure that they knew about the debacle from the previous year and that they were eagerly anticipating some equally juicy spectacle this year. Being a very slow learner, I reluctantly consented to try again. I was determined to make sure that no one knew the defendants or plaintiffs.

I called the case manager and asked about possible cases slated for the next few weeks and explained the fiasco from the previous year.

He said, "I've got the perfect case. Three young men have been arrested for stealing hubcaps. The police found the missing hubcaps in their car a block from the crime scene. There's an eyewitness and two of the three defendants have had numerous run-ins with the law. It looks like an air-tight case."

"Can you give me the names of the defendants?"

"Sure," he replied.

I went in the classroom the next day, wrote the three names on the board and asked if anyone recognized any of the three names.

No one did.

I was satisfied.

Once again, I rented the busses, got the permission slips, notified the other teachers of the planned absences and arranged for pickups if we did not get back to school in time to take the school busses home.

I was confident as we filed into the courtroom

and as the prosecution proceeded to present a seemingly open-and-shut case against the three young men in question.

All went well until the defense attorney called an alibi witness. She was—how shall we say—a "lady of the evening." She was dressed in a mini-skirt and a tube top and wore dangling earrings. She looked as if she had come straight from central casting.

She snapped her gum as she explained how it was totally impossible for any of the three to have been anywhere near the car on the night in question because she was "entertaining" them.

This lady was so crude and inappropriate that the judge kept telling her to watch her language.

My students were smirking and trying not to laugh but, at one point, the "lady" said something so outlandish that several of the students laughed.

The judge rapped the gavel and said, "I instruct the students to be quiet."

I put on my most serious teacher face and frowned at the offenders.

Several minutes later the lady crossed her legs and revealed what should have been covered with underpants. To my extreme horror and utter mortification, she was wearing nothing at all!

I immediately lost the whole front row to gasps, guffaws and giggles.

The judge rapped his gavel and said, "I am warning the teacher that the court will not abide this disruption."

At this point, I was so flustered that I just wanted out of that courtroom.

The defense attorney asked the witness how she could be sure that all three of the accused had been with her at the time that the crime allegedly had occurred.

She began to graphically explain what I can only describe as the "gymnastics" that she was performing with all three young men.

This time I lost the whole class. Even I, on the verge of a nervous breakdown and hysteria, started laughing.

In a voice filled with exasperation, the judge

rapped his gavel and said, "I order the teacher to remove her students from the courtroom."

We were removed from the courtroom for being disruptive, but I was never so glad to get thrown out of any place in my life!

I hustled those kids out of there as fast as I could. We boarded the bus and went directly back to school.

I walked into the office. In answer to the raised eyebrows of the school secretary and principal, I said, "Don't ask."

I never went back to court. My future students learned about trials from the film, *To Kill A Mockingbird.*

Ross

Every teacher knows that there are some students that you never forget. Sometimes they are the most unlikely of candidates. Ross fits into that category.

Ross was an uninspired ninth-grader who took up space in my classroom two periods a day, for Civics and English. With a mischievous grin, he would lope into the classroom, slink into his seat, crack jokes and be generally disruptive for the next fifty minutes.

The first time Ross really drew attention to himself was the second day of school.

I walked into my first hour class and, in large letters at the top of the chalkboard, it said, "Mrs. Bigler is a dope!"

I laughed and said, "Who's the one with the lousy penmanship?"

Ross laughed and said, "Guess who?"

"Mr. Royter, I presume?"

I strolled over to the board, erased "Mrs. Bigler" and wrote "Ross Royter."

We all laughed.

I left the statement on the board all hour.

Ross erased it on the way out.

When I walked into my fourth hour class, "Mrs. Bigler is a dope" graced the chalkboard again.

I erased my name and put in Ross'.

Thus began a routine that was to last all year. I occasionally questioned whether I was doing the right thing by allowing what some might consider disrespectful behavior. However, Ross was always affable and never insolent. To me, our exchanges always had the feel of harmless, good-natured ribbing, so we continued.

One day, Ross was out in the courtyard with his science class. I was teaching in my room. It was warm out so I had my windows open.

Ross came over and yelled in the window, "Mrs. Bigler is a dope."

I yelled back, "Ross Royter is a dope."

The class laughed.

Several minutes later there was a knock at my door. I opened the door to find the principal there with a solemn-looking Ross in tow.

"Mrs. Bigler, Ross has something to say to you."

"Mrs. Bigler, I want to apologize for interrupting your class." Ross was doing his best to sound sincere.

"And . . . " the principal coached.

"And for calling you a dope."

I felt terrible. I knew that the principal was trying to do his job. He had heard Ross yell and thought that Ross was being disrespectful. The principal did not know that this was a little game that we had played from the beginning of the school year. I wanted to tell him about it but I did not quite know how to " 'fess up" that I had been calling Ross a dope, too.

"Ross also has something he wants to say to your class," the principal continued.

"Oh, no. He's going to make Ross apologize to the class," I thought.

"All right," I replied.

Ross walked in the room.

The principal turned to go back to his duties.

Ross ambled to the front of the room and, with a twinkle in his eye, said, "Class, I would like to apologize for interrupting Mrs. Bigler's stimulating lecture. We all know that Mrs. Bigler is not a dope. Mrs. Bigler is an idiot."

The class burst out laughing.

The principal must not have been out of earshot of the laughter because he returned to the classroom and said, "Is there a problem?"

"Oh, no," I responded. "My class just has a good sense of humor."

On another occasion, I was walking down the stairs one day after school and stopped at the landing to look at the first significant snowfall of the season. I saw a bunch of kids throwing snowballs at each other. Although this was strictly against the rules, it rarely stopped anyone during the first snowfall.

I was standing there when Ross came into view. He was making a gigantic snowball.

I made a face at him.

He let the ball loose. It came at lightning speed and smacked violently against the window.

I almost jumped out of my skin! As soon as I collected myself, I determined that I was still in one piece but there was a substantial crack in the window. I motioned for Ross to come in. He did so immediately.

I said, "We've got to report this to the principal."

Ross agreed and we trudged to the office.

You have no idea how sheepish I felt telling the principal that Ross threw the snowball at me because I had been making faces at him. I felt like a third-grader, which was the last time I had been in a principal's office for disciplinary action (I had been reprimanded for picking flowers from my neighbor Beanie Stein's yard).

I don't think the principal knew what to do with us so he simply said, "Thank you for reporting it and don't do it again."

I'm not sure if he was talking to Ross, me or both of us. Nevertheless, we didn't do it again.

I left that school at the end of the school year and began teaching at the University. In early October, one of my graduate students approached me before class and handed me an envelope with my name on it.

I recognized the handwriting. How could I not after seeing it twice a day for 179 days?

"How do you know Ross Royter?" I asked.

"His mom and I play Bridge together. I was telling her about this class. When I said your name, she said, 'Oh, my gosh! Mrs. Bigler was Ross' all-time favorite teacher.' I guess his mom told Ross because, when we played Bridge Saturday, she asked me to give this to you from Ross."

I opened the letter.

Across the top, in big, bold letters, it said . . .

Well, you know what it said. Then Ross wrote, "The teachers at the high school don't have your sense of humor. I've been kicked out of class six times and it's only October!"

I called to thank Ross for his letter and encouraged him to improve his behavior and apply himself more. Of course, I hadn't gotten him to apply himself in a whole year's time, but to be a teacher is to never give up hope.

Ross called me intermittently throughout high school. Then, in January of his senior year, he called. The usually jovial Ross seemed very stressed out. He related that his parents were "applying pressure" to get him to attend college—any college.

Ross had absolutely no interest in going on to school. He loved working with his hands and wanted to go into the building trades.

This was not acceptable to his family. His dad was a college professor who intended for his son to go to college.

Ross said, "Mrs. Bigler, will you talk with

them? Make them understand I hate school. I've never liked school. I'd be miserable going to college. They don't listen to anything I say. They keep telling me that I have to go to college. Would you please talk to them?"

Although I made the usual teacher explanations to him about why his parents wanted him to continue with his schooling, I could not ignore the desperation in his voice.

"Okay, Ross. I hear you," I said. "Find out what's a good time for your parents and I'll come over. You'll need to have the courage of your convictions. This won't be easy, but you have to do what's right for you regardless of what anyone else thinks. That's what being an adult is all about. No one can live your life for you."

I arrived at the Royter home and Ross ushered me into the family room.

Over coffee, Mr. and Mrs. Royter, Ross and I talked about Ross and his future. I offered my view that Ross was a talented, personable young man who would do well in whatever he pursued. I expressed my opinion that college was not for everyone and that, if Ross ever needed more training or education, he could seek it out. In the meantime, I thought it was important for him to pursue his own dreams.

The Royters were gracious but unconvinced. Nevertheless, I felt that I had done the right thing by supporting Ross.

Six months later, Ross called and said that, although his parents were terribly disappointed that he was not going to college, they had made their peace with his decision. He had hired onto a crew that restored old homes. He was happy and making good money.

Eventually he went into business for himself traveling throughout the country restoring vintage homes.

He stayed in touch by calling or sending postcards several times a year.

I followed his career and was excited when he married and started his family.

Fifteen years and three children later, he called

me from Louisiana on a Sunday afternoon. We had been catching up on each other's lives for ten or fifteen minutes when I became concerned about the cost of the phone bill.

I said, "Ross, I always appreciate that you keep in touch. I am delighted that everything is going so well for you, but we'd better conclude this conversation or you're going to have to take on an extra job to pay your phone bill!"

He laughed and then hesitated.

"Mrs. Bigler . . . " His tone of voice had changed dramatically.

"Yes?" I responded.

"I want to tell you something."

Expecting him to announce another baby on the way or something of similar magnitude, I said, "Yes?"

"I love you."

Now, I don't know how many of you have thirty-two-year-old men calling you on the phone telling you that they love you or, for that matter, if you would even want that, but I was blown away. I was truly touched.

"Ross," I replied, "that's one of the nicest things anyone has ever said to me."

"Well, I got to thinking the other day that, if something happened to you before I had a chance to tell you how much you meant to me, I'd feel bad so I figured I had better tell you."

"I'm so glad that you did, Ross."

"Mrs. Bigler, do you remember when you came over to my parents' house to talk to them about me not wanting to go to college? You weren't even my teacher then, but you took the time to help me convince them I shouldn't go to college. You know, they still are disappointed that I didn't go. But, I've got a wonderful family, I love my work, I make good money, I contribute to my community and I try to be a good person. In my eyes, I am a success. I was never any kind of student. I know I did the right thing not going to college, but you were the only ally I had at that time in my life. Everyone else sided with my parents and nobody listened to

me. But you listened and that was awfully important to me. I don't know that I would have been
able to stand up to the onslaught from my relatives
and friends, but I kept hearing your voice saying,
'No one can live your life for you.' That's awfully
good advice. I've lived by it, so I want to thank you
for that. And, then, do you remember the snowball
incident?"

I laughed and said, "Oh, Ross, I'll never forget
that episode. I'm sure that's one of the memories
that I'll replay when I'm sitting in my rocker in the
nursing home."

"I've thought about it a lot. I think most teachers wouldn't have gone with me to the principal's
office. You walked right in there and said you were
partially to blame. I realize now that the principal
might have written you up or whatever it is they
do when teachers aren't acting professionally, but
you went right in there with me. That was too
cool, Mrs. Bigler, too cool."

What a privilege to be part of someone's life at a pivotal and life-altering moment. Teachers, we are richly blessed to share in, and contribute to, so many lives.

Danny

Danny was a likeable but lazy and disinterested student. No matter how hard I tried to engage him, nothing ever worked. Danny spent all his energy trying to figure out how to avoid work. It took me a while, but I finally came to see that Danny's lemons could make a little lemonade.

 Back in the days when teachers were still encouraged to have students memorize material, I used to ask my American History students to memorize the presidents of the United States in chronological order. I found that, if students identified events with a president's term and knew where that president came in the sequence of presidents, they could more readily place events in historical context.

Danny rarely did any of the assignments so you can imagine my surprise when, on the day of the presidents' test, Danny came in psyched to begin.

I stopped by his desk several times while I was monitoring the test. He was busily writing away.

I was proud that I had finally designed an assignment that he found engaging.

He was the first student to turn in his test.

I corrected his paper while I was waiting for everyone to finish. He had a perfect paper.

As the students were filing out of the room at the end of the period, I motioned for Danny to come to my desk.

When the last student had gone, I said, "Way to go, Danny! I am so proud of you. You earned an A on your presidents' test. You got them all right. See what you can do when you put your mind to it? You could be a top-notch student if you applied yourself like this every day."

The more I talked, the more uncomfortable

Danny became. He just looked down at the floor and did not say anything.

"How about it, Danny? Aren't you proud of yourself? This took a lot of discipline. You showed what you are made of today. I am so impressed!"

Embarrassed, Danny looked up and said, "I cheated, Mrs. Bigler."

Puzzled, I said, "Danny, you didn't cheat. I was watching you. Take credit for what you did. Be proud that you made this A."

"Mrs. Bigler, I *did* cheat."

With that, Danny removed a small tape recorder from his pocket and pushed the rewind button and played the tape aloud. It began, "George"—then the spelling—"capital G-e-o-r-g-e, Washington—capital W-a-s-h-i-n-g-t-o-n."

Sure enough, Danny had spelled all of the presidents' names on the tape. He had an earpiece that ran from his pocket to his right ear. Since he sat in the first row against the wall, I never would have discovered what he had done.

Impressed with his ingenuity and his confession

but disappointed with his cheating, I said, "Danny, it probably took you longer to make this tape than it would have to memorize the material in the first place."

"Yeah, but it wouldn't have been nearly as much fun as figuring out a way to get around the assignment," he responded.

Danny started me thinking. He helped me realize that it takes industry and imagination to create ways to beat the rules. In fact, in the real world, people are often rewarded for their daring and originality. Creative and resourceful people become inventors and entrepreneurs. The challenge for us is to help the Dannys of the world to employ their talents in appropriate, ethical and productive ways. We must show these students ways to have more fun and fulfillment learning than they have breaking the rules.

Mike

Teacher and poet Mark Van Doren said,
"The art of teaching is the art of assisting
discovery." Mike and I assisted each other
in discovery.

Mike was a troubled adolescent. His senior
year of high school was a tough time for
him and for his teachers.

I caught him cheating on a test.

In those days, we thought that the best way to
discourage cheaters was to embarrass them in
front of their peers. So, I directed Mike to tear his
paper up in front of his classmates and made a
production of putting a zero in the grade book.

He became angry and told me to stick it where

the sun didn't shine but in much more graphic terms.

I sent him to the principal's office.

He was suspended from school for three days and would have been expelled if I had not intervened. I asked that he be given another chance since graduation was only a few months off.

He was given another chance.

He graduated from high school. I have to say that we were not sad to see this belligerent and cocky young man go.

Mike joined the Marines and went to Vietnam.

He came home on leave one December and showed up at my classroom door. He looked like a million bucks in his uniform.

I gave my class an assignment and stood in the hall visiting with him.

"Mrs. Bigler, I came back to tell you something," he said.

I thought that he was going to thank me for intervening on his behalf before graduation. Instead he said, "I want you to know that something you said has really made a difference in my life. You know how I used to flip off at the end of the films?"

How could I forget? When I showed the old sixteen-millimeter films, there were several seconds of white light on the screen at the end of the films. Some of the boys would sit by the projector so they could raise their middle finger and garner some laughs from the other boys.

"I used to do that all the time," Mike continued. "I suppose you got tired of calling me on it. But, one time, you said, 'Mike, before you say or do anything, why don't you look around the room? Ask yourself if anyone would be offended by what you might do or say. If they could be, just don't do or say it.' "

"I've got to tell you. Many, many times before I do or say something, I look around the barracks, the room or the bar and I ask myself, would anyone be offended? If I think even one person might be, I don't say or do it. I can't tell you how many things I haven't said or done because of that. That advice has kept me out of more fights than I care to think about. I wanted to tell you to keep telling other students that because, Mrs. Bigler, it's the best piece of advice I've ever been given."

I thanked Mike for sharing that with me. I was smiling to myself thinking that I didn't even remember saying that to him.

I invited him to come into the class and talk about his experiences in the military. He talked for fifteen or twenty minutes, answered questions from the class and then prepared to leave.

He turned to me and said, "Mrs. Bigler, I can't leave without saying something else. I need to apologize for what I said to you my senior year. I can't take the words back, but I can tell you I'm sorry for what I said."

"Mike, your apology is accepted, but I want to apologize to you, too. I mishandled the situation. I wouldn't do today what I did then. I should have handled that situation privately. I backed you into a corner and you struck out. So we've both learned."

The students had no idea what we were talking

about, but they realized that reconciliation had occurred.

He gave me a hug and a smile.

I watched proudly as this wise and mature young man walked out the door. That was the last time I saw Mike.

He died in Vietnam.

I helped Mike learn about consideration and self-discipline. He helped me learn that we all make mistakes but that we can learn from them and be better human beings than we were before.

Mr. K,
the Math Principal

Mr. K had been a junior high math teacher for many years before he became an elementary building principal at our neighborhood school. If you told people in our town where your children went to school, they would say, "Oh, you have Mr. K, the math principal." I heard "Mr. K, the math principal" so many times that I thought that was his name!

Do you know why Mr. K was called the math principal? Because Mr. K loved math and everybody who knew him knew that.

I used to hate to walk down the halls with Mr. K because he would stop and give a math problem to every student he encountered. If it was a kindergartner, he might say, "What is one plus one?" If it was a fifth-grader, he might say, "What is ¼ plus ¼?" If he didn't offer a math problem, the children would ask him for one. They would tug on his sleeve and say, "Mr. K, you haven't given us a math problem yet." I'm telling you, it used to take twenty minutes to reach the first classroom if you were with Mr. K!

Do you think there was any doubt in the minds of the staff, students or parents at that school what Mr. K's academic priorities were? Mr. K loved and valued math and everyone knew it.

What do you love and value? If you say language arts, I'll bet more of your students like language arts than anything else in the curriculum. If you love teaching science, I'll bet most of your kids love science. If we teach what we love and value, we can usually get kids to love and value it, too. That's an important lesson learned from Mr. K, a remarkable principal and an ardent lover of math.

Darius and Jon

Teachers know that the students who need us
the most are often the students from whom
we learn the most. I learned a great deal from
Darius and Jon.

Darius and Jon were a pair! My principal
said that they were a challenge. I had other
words to describe them. Talkative, lazy, and indif-
ferent are some of the more positive adjectives that
I could use, although rude, insolent and disgusting
might be more accurate. They really were not bad
kids. They were mischievous and looked for ways to
get attention like having burping contests, putting
whoopie cushions on their seats and releasing six
garter snakes in class while a test was being given.

They egged each other on and delighted in getting a rise out of me. They tried my patience fifty times in fifty minutes. I have to admit that I dreaded fourth-hour American History because nothing that I tried worked to settle them down.

One particularly bad day I lost it. I mean, I *really* lost it. I don't know if it was because of Darius or Jon or if it was the one-two combination, but I lost my temper. Now, we all know that we can't lose our tempers when we teach because we are apt to say and do things that are unreasonable. Before I knew what I was saying, I yelled, "You two will not be allowed back in this class until you write, in order, the first and last names of the presidents of the United States, five hundred times!"

As soon as I said it, I knew that I was way off base. What was I teaching? I was teaching that learning the presidents is a punishment and that writing is a punishment. It went against everything that I believed but I'm telling you that it was out of my mouth before I even realized it.

I wanted to retract what I had said but, when you are an inexperienced teacher, you think that you will lose credibility if you do that. I wanted them to know that I meant business so I let the punishment stand.

I felt terrible. I knew that I was wrong but I did not have the confidence to say, "Look, guys, I am sorry. The punishment is not appropriate. Let's think of something else that we might do to help you establish limits in here."

I felt sheepish all evening.

The phone rang around 9:30 that night. It was Darius' mom. "Mrs. Bigler, I want to be supportive of you. I know Darius is a handful. He has been writing the presidents ever since he came home and he has over 200. I wanted to ask if he could please come back to class tomorrow. I assure you he will continue to work on the assignment until all 500 are done but I hate for him to miss class because he is already behind."

"Oh, Mrs. Taylor, I am so glad you called. I feel terrible about this whole situation. I lost my temper and gave an unreasonable punishment. Tell Darius to stop writing now. Whatever he has is sufficient. He can return to class tomorrow and perhaps we can all meet and discuss what he can do to not be so disruptive."

I hung up the phone and thought, "Here's a mother who is trying to back me up, even when I am over the top. I have got to do better with Darius."

I did not know how to contact Jon. The next morning I arrived at school early, found his phone number and called him. I told him that whatever he had done was sufficient and that he could come back to class. He did not show up. He came the following day with all 500 spellings of the presidents, in order, first and last names.

I said, "Jon, I told you that whatever you had done was enough. You didn't have to do anymore. Why did you do this?"

"My dad said I had to," he muttered.

(Talk about parental support!)

I would like to report that Darius and Jon

changed their ways and became model students, but they did not. However, we all survived.

At a recent class reunion they made me painfully aware that our bad deeds are never forgotten when they entertained their classmates with *their* version of "The 500 Presidents' Assignment."

Over the years I have learned that young people understand that teachers are human. They respect honesty and appreciate our efforts to treat them fairly. I have also learned that you have to have the honesty to admit when you have made a mistake and the courage to right the wrong as soon as possible.

Senior Advisor

Of all the thankless jobs, being a class advisor has to rank at the top of the list. But being the *senior* class advisor is the absolute pits! Whether riding herd on over-amorous couples at the prom, pleading for some unwitting family to host the building of the homecoming float or arguing with the students that "Up Yours" is not an appropriate class motto, I found the possibilities for migraines to be endless. Among the most harrowing of responsibilities is being in charge of graduation.

With a full awareness of the importance of this momentous occasion for the Seniors, their families and fellow students and with a clear understanding that the smooth functioning of this event reflected well on the school, I, as you can well imagine, was filled with tremendous relief on the afternoon of graduation as I left the building confident that everything was ready for the happy celebration at eight o'clock that night.

All was well until about 5:00 p.m. Preparing for the auspicious event, I was taking a shower.

It came in a flash. "Oh, no! I forgot to order flowers for the stage!"

I panicked. Could graduation occur without flowers gracing the stage? Isn't there some imperative handed down from past generations that says that there must be flowers on the stage for graduation?

It was 5:00 p.m. Where could I get flowers in time for graduation? Dripping wet but hoping to find one of the floral shops still open, I ran downstairs and grabbed the phonebook.

I dialed three florists and did not get an answer at any of them. With the flowers shops closed, where could I find sprays of spring flowers after five o'clock at night?

I was desperate.

Another flash—Divine Inspiration—a funeral home!

I started calling funeral homes and pleading my case. The first person hung up on me, the second sympathized but was unwilling to help and the third started laughing.

I found a friend at the fourth home. I begged for two large sprays that would grace either side of the stage.

The funeral home employee said, "If you promise never to tell anyone I did this, you can come up the back alley behind the home and I will give you two sprays. However, they must be returned tonight because they are from a viewing scheduled for 9:00 a.m. tomorrow."

I promised on my unborn first child that I would personally return them that night. I drove like a madwoman to the funeral home, got the sprays, took them to school, arranged them on the stage and hurried to the choir room to help the Seniors with their robes.

Graduation proceeded without a hitch. I sat congratulating myself on my resourcefulness. It did occur to me that someone at the graduation might be attending a viewing in the morning and might think that the flowers there resembled the flowers from graduation the night before, but I truly had no energy to worry about it at that time.

After all the hugs, kisses and picture taking, the kids headed out to the various parties.

I, ulterior motives in mind, volunteered to help the custodians clean up the debris. My agenda was to get the sprays back in my car.

When the custodian saw me, he said, "I'll get those, Mrs. Bigler. I always deliver them to Fountain View."

The school donated flowers to the local nursing home after events of this kind. I had forgotten about that.

"Oh, that's all right," I said. "The Seniors voted to take them someplace else this year." (Being Senior Advisor teaches you to lie.)

"Where?" he asked.

"The hospital," I answered.

"Oh," he said. "Well, I'll drop them off there, then."

"Thank you, but that's not necessary, Mr. Williams. It's right on my way home."

He helped me load them into the car.

I took them straight back to the funeral home. I offered my profound thanks and went home.

In the middle of the summer, I received a call from my principal. "Mrs. Bigler, this is Mr. Yoder. I wanted to check with you about the graduation flowers. We never received a bill for them from the florist. I called The Petal Shop" (the florist the school traditionally dealt with) "and they said that we didn't order any flowers from them for gradua-tion. I know that must be a mistake so I need you to help me sort this out."

As smoothly as if I had been lying profusely all my life, I said, "Oh, we didn't get them from The Petal Shop. I have a good friend who works at Flower Power and she donated the flowers for graduation."

"How very kind," said Mr. Yoder. "Do give me her name so that I can write a thank-you letter on behalf of the school."

"I've taken care of that, Mr. Yoder. I wrote a lovely thank-you note and signed it, 'Staff and Students'."

"Thank you, Mrs. Bigler. You are so efficient! I so very much appreciate your efforts as Senior Class Advisor. Would you be willing to do it again next year?"

Arlen

As a teacher, I usually want to learn all that I can about my students. But there have been times when I've been intimidated by what I've discovered.

One summer I was offered the opportunity to teach in a program for gifted children. Knowing that I would be working with very bright young people, I realized that I needed to become more knowledgeable to support them in their learning. I read numerous articles, talked to colleagues who had worked in similar programs and visited with my professors.

One suggestion that I received was that I should not make value judgments that might discourage the students from being creative. Taking this advice to heart, I resolved to be as open to the responses of my students as I could be.

I approached the first day of class with anticipation and confidence. That lasted about an hour! The very first assignment that I gave was for the students to make a collage of what they wanted out of life. I thought that would be a good opening activity. It would allow me to get to know the students better and give me insights into what they valued.

The students eagerly started cutting out pictures from the magazines that I had brought to class. They pasted their pictures and wrote their ideas on construction paper. When they had finished, they brought their posters to me to review before presenting them to the class.

Arlen approached me with his collage. He had neatly arranged pictures of astronauts, the moon, rockets and space. But the most intriguing aspect of his collage was that he had "The Future" upside down at the bottom of the collage.

He handed me his collage.

I briefly looked at the pictures and then turned the collage upside down to read the title. I was mystified by what he was conveying but, cautious of not wanting to squelch his creativity with value judgments, I took the easy way out and said, "This is interesting."

He didn't respond so I said, "This is *really* interesting." I put lots of oomph on "really" so that he wouldn't realize that I didn't know what else to say.

He did not respond.

"Arlen, I find your collage *most* interesting," I tried again.

He said nothing.

Finally, in desperation, I thought, "Hey, I don't care if I discourage his creativity. I don't have the foggiest notion of what message Arlen is trying to convey. I'm just going to ask him."

So, I said, "Arlen, I'm not sure that I understand what you are saying here. Do you want things to be upside down, confused, topsy-turvy?"

He replied, "Mrs. Bigler, I thought you wanted us to make a collage about what we want out of life."

"That's right, Arlen, but that's what I don't understand. It looks like you want to be an astronaut or part of the space industry or something but I don't know why the title is upside down. Is that supposed to represent how the earth looks from space?" (I was rather pleased with this observation.)

"No, Mrs. Bigler. I don't care anything about the space program. What I want is power over people. I just programmed you. I knew, when I handed the collage to you, you would turn it upside down to read the title. So I just controlled you. That's power!"

I was speechless. I really was. The expression, "My blood ran cold," comes to mind. Arlen had handed me his collage and I did exactly what he had wanted. I had turned it upside down. I had just been programmed by an eleven-year-old! The realization that I had to spend the summer with a boy who wanted power over people was more than intimidating. It was downright scary!

> The summer program was a tremendous learning opportunity for me. I have reflected on it often in my career. I learned to never underestimate the thinking, both positive and negative, that students can do. I learned that we have students with interests, desires, abilities and knowledge that can be used productively or destructively. I strove to help Arlen and the other students develop their cognitive and affective strengths so that they could put their talents to use in making the world a better place. We have to make sure that the future leaders sitting in our classrooms today become leaders that will use their "power" to improve the quality of life for others tomorrow.

Lateesha

Never underestimate the importance of a parent reading to a child.

I have usually found parent-teacher conferences to be pleasant and beneficial. Occasionally they are frustrating or puzzling. The most confusing was my conference with Lateesha's mom. She completely surprised me by expressing her concerns about Lateesha's reading.

"Mrs. Bigler, I don't understand why Lateesha is having so much trouble reading. Her two older sisters are excellent readers. I've read to all the girls since they were little. I can't understand why Lateesha can't read."

I was bewildered. Lateesha was one of the best

readers in the third grade. I couldn't imagine what her mom was talking about. So I asked, "What makes you think that Lateesha is having trouble reading? What does she do that makes you think that she is not a good reader?"

Her mom said, "Well, I'm not a reading expert or anything, but it's obvious Lateesha is having trouble. She doesn't read with any expression. She reads word-by-word. She ignores punctuations marks. When she comes to a word she doesn't know, she doesn't try to sound it out or skip it. She just stops. When she's done reading, I ask her questions about what she's read and she can't answer the questions. I mean, I don't know what you want me to say, but it is clear she can't read well."

I am not often at a loss for words but, I have to tell you, I was completely dumbfounded. I could not think of anything to say to her. I finally managed, "Let me get back to you on this."

The next morning when Lateesha arrived, I said, "Lateesha, I need to talk with you."

She came to my desk.

"Why does your mom think that you aren't a good reader?" I asked.

"Oh, no! Mrs. Bigler, you didn't tell her I can read did you?" she pleaded.

"I did not. But why does she think that you are not a good reader?"

"Please, Mrs. Bigler, you didn't tell her I could read did you?"

"No, but I need to know why your mom thinks that you have trouble with reading."

"Well," she began rather sheepishly, "my sisters said that, if Mom knows I can read, she will quit reading to us. They said she quit reading to them when they learned to read. So they said I should just pretend I can't read and then she'll keep reading to us."

I had to hide a smile as I asked, "What do you do to make your mom think that you can't read?"

"Oh, I just do what you tell us *not* to do or else I don't do what you tell us *to* do, Mrs. Bigler. I don't read with expression. I ignore the punctuation marks. I read real slow and word by word and, when I come to a hard word, I just stop like I don't know what to do and, when Mom asks me questions about what I read, I just pretend I don't know the answers."

I was so surprised. I said, "Lateesha, I don't want your mom worrying about your reading so can we make a deal? I want you to go home this afternoon and I want you to read for your mom just as well as you read here at school. Now I'll get your mom to promise that she will continue reading to you even if you read very well. Do we have a deal?"

"I'll have to ask my sisters," she replied.

"Fair enough," I said, laughing to myself.

She went out for recess, talked to her sisters and came back to me and said, "Okay. We have a deal."

I called her mom and said, "You really caught me off guard last night. When you were so concerned about Lateesha's reading, I was confused because she is one of the best third grade readers that I have ever had. I just couldn't believe what you were telling me so I had a conversation with her this morning and let me tell you what she told me."

The mother listened to my explanation and said, "I can hardly believe this."

I said, "I know what you mean. I couldn't believe what you said to me last night, so I'm sure you are just as confused as I was. I've taught for many years and this is the first time that I've heard this one. I can assure you that Lateesha is a good reader and that she's going to prove it to you when she gets home this afternoon."

I received a phone call from Lateesha's mom about 4:30 that afternoon. She said, "I can't believe this. Who would think kids would hatch a plot like this? I am delighted Lateesha is reading so well and I promise I'll keep reading to the girls."

"You'd better or my reputation is shot," I laughed.

Never underestimate children. My students know lots of things that I surely do not. They know how to get the utilities turned back on, how to program their iPods and how to get their moms to keep reading to them!

Also, never underestimate the truth of the American poet Strickland Gillilan's old saying, "Richer than I you can never be, for I had a mother who read to me."

The Filing Cabinet

I offer this story to you as a cautionary tale about the dangers of filing cabinets.

I was teaching night classes at the University as an adjunct instructor in the early 70's. I had a tiny office in a suite of offices with walls that did not reach to the ceiling.

One night I finished teaching, returned to my office, shut the door and opened the second drawer of my four-drawer filing cabinet. Without closing the open drawer, I opened the top drawer.

The filing cabinet tilted forward pinning me against the back wall right in front of the door. I was unharmed but the filing cabinet pressed right above my breasts so my arms were pinned at my sides. It was nine-thirty at night. No one else would be coming into the suite until the next morning.

Luckily there was an umbrella behind the door that I could reach with my right hand. I maneuvered it into my left hand. I pulled the cord on the phone with the handle of the umbrella and the phone fell to the floor.

I pulled the phone to the filing cabinet where I was able to push the numbers with the tip of the umbrella. I called Campus Security.

When someone answered, I yelled, "This is Mary Bigler. I am trapped in my office on the third floor of Pierce Hall. The filing cabinet fell on me. I am okay but I can't move. I have the door blocked so whoever comes will have to climb over the top of the wall to get into the office."

The officer said, "Well, that's a new one! You're lucky you aren't hurt. I'll send two security officers over immediately."

In a matter of minutes, I heard keys in the outer door.

Someone yelled, "Campus Security! Where are you?"

"Office F," I replied.

I heard two voices discussing how to enter the adjoining office and scale the wall into my office.

When the first man came over the wall, I was taken aback. He looked more like a street person than a security officer. If I had met him in a dark alley, I would have been afraid. He must have sensed my trepidation because he immediately announced that he was an undercover security officer. (I did not even know that the University employed undercover security officers.)

They tried to lift the cabinet off me, but they could not get any leverage. They could only work from one side because the cabinet was up against the wall and the door was on the other side.

The smaller of the two men blushed, "Lady, this is rather embarrassing but I need to get between you and the filing cabinet, so I'm going to have to crawl between your legs and the cabinet."

I braced myself, "Do what you have to do."

I frankly don't know who was more uncomfortable, the officer or I, but he squeezed into the small space between me and the base of the filing cabinet. Then he pushed on the filing cabinet from below while his partner pushed and pulled from above. They succeeded in getting it upright.

Every time that I open a drawer in a filing cabinet I think of how lucky I was that night. I am sure my colleagues have wearied of me reminding them to close their file drawers. I am equally sure that those security officers are still regaling their fellow workers with the tale of the falling filing cabinet fiasco.

Dog Pooh

Teacher preparation courses can never prepare you for the myriad situations that you
will encounter when you teach.

During the sweltering summer of 1972, I
was teaching a reading class at the University. In the middle of my lecture, a large Doberman
pinscher entered the room. Although it was highly
discouraged, it was not unusual for students to
bring dogs to class in those days.

I asked if he belonged to someone in the class.

No one claimed him.

About that time, the dog walked to the center
of the room and answered the call of nature and I
do not mean a small call.

As the students were guffawing and groaning, I was thinking that none of my methods classes had prepared me for this. Just what was I supposed to do?

One of my students volunteered, "I'll take care of it. I have dogs. I'm used to cleaning up after them."

With my profound thanks and undying gratitude, she left the room to get paper towels.

I tried to carry on as if everything was normal.

The young lady returned and began cleaning up the sizable pile when she started to gag. In the next few seconds, we had a coating of vomit on the dog pooh pile. The young lady was terribly embarrassed and fled the room.

I directed the other students to leave the room and wait in the hall.

I hurried to the Department Head's office and explained to the secretary that I had a situation in my class.

The Department Head heard me and poked his head out of his office.

"What's wrong, Mary?"

Now the Department Head was a very refined gentleman. I did not have the courage to blurt out that I had dog pooh and vomit on my floor so I said, "I need to have another classroom."

"Why?" he asked.

"There's a problem with my room."

"What's the problem?"

There was nothing to do but to tell him. "Well, a dog came in and made a mess. Then one of my students got sick trying to clean it up so now we have two messes. It smells. I don't think that it's conducive to learning."

"Whose dog is it?" asked the Department Head.

"I don't know. It doesn't belong to any of my students," I responded.

"What kind of a dog is it?"

I told him. Then he asked for a description and I gave him one.

In an agitated tone of voice he said, "I know whose dog it is and he will clean it up!"

The dog belonged to one of the professors! The

Department Head went to the professor's office and got him.

The professor cleaned up the mess while we were moved to another room where I finished the class without further incident.

None of my education professors ever told me that students would knock on the door while I was in the bathroom to ask me to open their thermos bottles. No one ever told me to keep an extra pair of kid's jeans for the occasional "accident" that occurs in every primary classroom. No one ever told me that a mother would ask me to take a stool sample from her child because she didn't know how to do it. And no one ever told me what to do when a dog answers the call of nature in the middle of my classroom!

Teacher Want Ads

If you'd like to find out what your students *really* think of you, try this assignment. Now, don't do this in January. Wait until the end of the school year because it can be very deflating. About a week before school is over, at the time when all the students are speculating about whose class they are going to be in next year, assign them to write a want ad for their ideal teacher.

Of course, everything they want in the new teacher is what I am not and everything they do not want is what I am! So I know exactly what I am going to get. The kids complain all year about my shortcomings so the ads contain no surprises for me. I let them write their brutally honest ads.

Then I get up in front of the group and read them aloud.

I have more fun with this assignment than any other. I have done it with every age level.

My tenth graders were rolling in the aisles when I read Rivka's:

Wanted: One new teacher! Thin!

(What do you mean "thin"? Don't you like what you've got?)

One who doesn't talk so fast.

(My kids don't call me The Fastest Gums in the West for nothing!)

One who's not so enthusiastic
about everything.

(My tenth-graders used to come in and say, "Mrs. Bigler, can't we just do something *boring* today?" or "Mrs. Bigler, you're great for an hour, but we can't take you much longer than that!")

One who doesn't say, "This is
fun," all the time.

(You know how kids pick up on anything you over-use. Well, I always say "fun." "This is *fun*." "We're going to have *fun* today." "Wasn't that *fun*?")

After I had read all of the want ads aloud and the kids were thinking that this had been the most fun (there I go again) that they had had all year, I dramatically opened the bottom drawer of my desk and pulled out several sheets of paper.

The kids asked what I was doing and I said, "Well, if you get to write a want ad for a new teacher, I get to write a want ad for a new class."

"You can't do that!" they protested, but they couldn't wait to hear what my want ad said.

I began, "I want a class where Clemencia and Colin aren't passing notes all hour. I want a class where Casey returns her library books on time. I want a class where Tyrone remembers to put his name on his paper, . . . " I continued until I had included every student's name and what they had done to aggravate me all year.

The absolute best want ads are from the little ones. You might not think that first-graders know what they want in their teacher but I am here to tell you that they do and they are articulate.

Chrissy writes:

> *Wanted: New teacher. Must be*
> *dressed neat. Must wear a*
> *dress on Friday. Must wear a*
> *skirt on Tuesday.*

(When you teach first grade, you are on the floor half the time. So, of course, the kids want you in a skirt. Go figure!)

> *Must wear lipstick everyday*

(I couldn't wait to run right down and show this to the other first grade teacher, *Mister* Benson.)

> *and must not yell.*

Brad writes:

> *Wanted: Man. Must be strong.*
> *Must be smart. Must not get*
> *hurt. Must eat food. Must drink*
> *drinks. Must have brain. Must be*
> *29 years old.*

(That sounds like *my* want ad!)

Ahmad writes:

> *Wanted: Teacher. Must be young
> and nice. Have experience and
> good health and take you on
> field trips. Must never be absent
> and must be able to see well and
> smell well and hear well.*

Then there is Sarah. Sarah was not one of my favorite people. I am a little suspicious of teachers who say, "I love all the children." If you do, I salute you. But I can't honestly say I *love* all the children. In fact, there are usually a couple that I don't even *like*! I work hard all year camouflaging that. I work my heart out for every child that I am given, but I cannot say that I love them all. A teacher friend of mine has the greatest line that I ever heard. She says, "If you've taught school more than five years, you should never have children of your own because you won't be able to name them." Well, I would never name my daughter Sarah. (Sarah wasn't too fond of me, either!)

Here's Sarah's want ad:

> *Wanted: Female teacher. Must be in late 20's. Must not weigh over 150 pounds. Must have long brown hair. Must wear dresses only. Must bring Popsicles for a snack every day. Must have Master's degree.*

Then there's Letitia. She says:

> *Wanted: Teacher to work!*

(I love this want ad. I told my first-graders that, when I got home from work, I liked to cook. Cedric said, "Oh! Where do you work?")

The absolute best want ad is from Javon. She has the best phrase to describe a teacher that I have ever heard. If you work with little ones, you will grasp this immediately. If you work with older students, you don't hear this as much, but I'll explain it.

Javon says:

> *Wanted: Teacher. Must be lady.*

Must be nice. Must be smart.
Must be experienced. Must have
short hair. Must wear pants
every Monday. Must know how to
spell. And must KNOW WHAT
IT IS.

You know when you work with kindergarten and first grade children, they create a picture and bring it to your desk and you have no idea what it is. Now we all took educational psychology. We know what we are supposed to say: "Tell me about it." But let's be honest. After you have had twenty-five papers cross your desk that don't resemble anything close to reality, you forget the educational psychology and you say, "WHAT IS IT?" Little Javon wants a teacher who "KNOWS WHAT IT IS." I think that is the best description of a teacher that I have ever heard.

Margaret

One of the most important lessons that I have learned in over forty years of teaching is to respect the differences in my colleagues. Now, I know that may sound funny, but let me explain.

In the early years of my teaching career, I thought I was a terrific teacher. I really did. I thought, if all the teachers just taught like me, we wouldn't have any problems. How's that for humility? Well, it's what I thought. I mean, I had my kids *pumped*! We ran to the library, went on exotic field trips, put on plays. We did it all.

But, for the whole school year, I was sick to my stomach. Do you know why? Because, come September, I knew my kids would have to leave my stimulating classroom and go across the hall to boring, dull, old Margaret.

Now, you just think of the most boring individual you have ever encountered. Multiply that by ten million and you will have an idea about Margaret. Some of the other teachers said, "Margaret's not so bad. She's just laid back."

"Laid back!" I almost screamed. "She's laid out!" I mean the woman was deadly. I was sick at the thought of having to send my kids to her.

But, let me tell you the truth. No matter how good I thought I was—and I was good for a lot of the students—there were at least three children in that class that I never quite reached. I left no stone unturned to try to engage those children but, in my heart of hearts, I knew that I was not the best teacher for them. I did not give them what they needed. I never gave up on them but I did not succeed with them, either.

Well, September came and my class went across the hall to boring, dull, old Margaret. But, you know how it is when your class leaves you.

They are still yours. You follow them. So I watched those kids.

And, do you know what I discovered about six weeks into the new school year? Of course, you do. You know those three? Do you know what happened when they got over with the most boring individual that I have ever encountered? They started to blossom. BLOSSOM! They blossomed with the most boring teacher that I had ever known. Boy, did that made me angry! I was so good but I could not get out of those kids what boring, dull, old Margaret could.

Once I calmed down, I began to realize that Margaret had gifts to give that I would never have. Margaret was about as different from me as any one could be. Margaret was quiet. When I talked, the windows rattled. (Margaret would go to the principal and say, "I'd prefer not to teach next to Mary Bigler. She's so loud." Can you believe that she said that about me? I wanted to say, "I'd prefer not to teach next to Margaret. She's so boring." But, of course, I didn't say it.) Margaret was patient. I mean, you have never seen anyone as patient as Margaret. She could wait three weeks for an answer! I wanted everything answered and done . . . yesterday. Margaret was sweet—syrupy sweet. I hate sweet! Margaret was gentle. If you thought of a hundred adjectives to describe Mary Bigler, "gentle" would not be on the list.

I came to realize that Margaret was a refuge from . . . me! I overwhelmed and intimidated some kids—not that I wanted to. It's just that I'm a type A, high-energy personality and that comes through when I teach. And that's great for a lot of kids—just not for all kids. Margaret taught me that there is no one teacher who reaches all the students.

Today, when children leave my classroom, I pray they go to Margaret. You see, I have given them my best. Now Margaret will give them her best. If we all give our best, the students are the beneficiaries and are enriched by our differences.

Bill

I would like to share a story with you that speaks to the power of expectations more than any other story that I know. It is about a good man—my husband, Bill.

Bill was the product of a single-parent home back in the days when divorce was virtually unheard of and when it carried a serious social stigma. He grew up as an only child, with no father in his life and with a single working mother who did the best that she could to raise him.

By the time he got into seventh and eighth grades, he started getting into trouble in school for the kinds of activities that young people continue to get into trouble for doing—things like tardiness, truancy, talking, clowning around in class, etc. Now, if you knew Bill today, you would find that hard to believe because he's such a straight arrow. But junior high was a tough time for him.

One day, when Bill was a big, brassy eighth-grader, he got kicked out of class for the "umpteenth" time and had to report to the vice-principal's office. (Principal of Vice. What a job!) The vice-principal was in charge of discipline. Bill was not a stranger to his office. The vice-principal's secretary told Bill that the vice-principal was not in the building and that he would have to go down the hall to the principal's office.

Bill wasn't intimidated by that! He and the principal were on a first-name basis. He strutted on down to the principal's office. The secretary asked why he was there.

He explained that he had been kicked out of class and that the vice-principal was not in the building so he had been instructed to report to the principal's office. The principal's secretary responded that the principal was also out of the building and told Bill that he would have to go across the street and speak to the high school principal.

Going to see the high school principal *was* scary, even for a big, cocky eighth-grader. But, when you are a tough guy, you don't let anyone know that you are intimidated. So Bill strolled across the street and sauntered into the high school principal's office.

The secretary asked, "Who are you?"

"I'm Bill Bigler. I've been kicked out of class at the junior high school and the vice-principal and principal are gone and I'm supposed to see the high school principal."

The secretary went into the principal's office and returned a few moments later and said, "Okay. He'll see you now."

Bill walked into the high school principal's office. Before I tell you what the man said, I want to tell you what he did not say. He did not say, "Why are you here?" or "What have you done?" In fact, he made no reference at all as to why Bill was there. Instead, that gentleman stood up, extended his right hand and said, "Bill Bigler, I've been hearing a lot about you." (I bet!) "I'm really glad we are having this opportunity to get acquainted. I understand you are bright, a good athlete and a leader."

Incidentally, that was all true. Bill was bright. His grades were not stellar because he was undisciplined and unmotivated unless he found particular interest or enjoyment in a given assignment. He was a good athlete and well liked by his classmates. He was a natural leader but not interested in assuming the formal roles of leadership in school.

The principal continued, "Bill, I am really looking forward to having you join us here at the high school next year. I am sure that you are going to make many contributions to our school and I just want you to know, Bill, that I am expecting great things from you."

This was a life-altering event for Bill. He had never had anyone at school say such things to him.

They usually addressed what he was doing wrong—not what he was doing right. He had never had any adults tell him that they expected great things from him.

As Bill sat in that office, he thought to himself, "You are screwing up! You are doing nothing. You are going nowhere. You have to shape up. This man expects something out of you." Then and there he made the decision that he would never again be in a principal's office for anything that he was doing wrong. He never was.

Bill went on to high school. He sang in the choir, starred in the junior and senior plays, was a three-year varsity center on the football team, center on the basketball team, track team participant, chess champion, editor of the yearbook, president of the honor society, class president, president of the student council, and president of the inter-league student council. Bill Bigler graduated number one, valedictorian, of his high school class!

If you have to do a disservice to a young person, do it on the side of expecting too much as opposed to settling for too little. If you want your students to be good, find the goodness within them. If you want your students to do great things, expect great things from them.

Dad and Mom

My father (the teacher) and my mother (the speaker) were wonderful, loving parents who taught me many valuable life lessons, two of which follow.

*Our reputations follow
us through life.*

Ernest Dean Glenn

*You've got to bloom
where you're planted.*

Maxine Dermody Glenn

Dad

Most of the time we receive our inheritances late in life. I was fortunate enough to receive one of mine early.

When I was nine years old, my dad dropped me off at the grocery store in our little Iowa town. I was supposed to buy some milk and bread, but I had a problem. I had forgotten to take the money that he had given me to pay for it.

When I reached the counter, I explained to the owner of the store that I did not have any money.

He said that was fine because my dad would pay for it the next time he came in.

As I was leaving the store, one of the old-timers who had gathered with his buddies for their morning conversation and coffee jokingly said to the grocer, "Geez, I wish you'd let *me* take stuff out of here without paying for it."

The grocer responded, "That's Ernie Glenn's daughter. Ernie's good for it. He's the most honest man in Benton County."

The farmer looked at me and said, "Little girl, your dad has given you a wonderful legacy to live up to. Don't you forget it."

I never have forgotten it. My dad valued honesty, fairness, and responsibility above all else. He taught me that our reputations follow us through life and that we should steer a straight course if we expect people to trust us.

I have tried to live my life by Dad's credo. I have also tried to model it for, and impart it to, my students. I hope Dad's story will help us all to instill honesty, fairness and responsibility in our students.

Mom

We often learn best when our teacher holds our hand, but once in a while we require a kick in another part of our anatomy.

I was miserably unhappy after my family moved to Michigan in the middle of my sophomore year. For five months I cried every night and begged to move back to Iowa. I did not try to make friends, I did not care about my classes and I was mad at everyone who had put me in this awful situation.

All that time my mother and dad were patient and sympathetic but, by May, my mother had had enough.

One night she came into my bedroom. I was

sitting with swollen eyes and a box of Kleenex. She was all business. She said, "Mary, we are not moving back to Iowa. You have two choices. You can wallow in self-pity for the rest of your high school career or you can decide to make the best of the situation. As far as I am concerned, you need to 'bloom where you are planted' but you will have to decide if you are going to do that or not."

She turned around and marched out of the room.

I was extremely perplexed. My mom was as patient, gracious, kind, warm-hearted and loving a person as I had ever known. Ever since we had moved, she had been completely sympathetic to me. She had been telling me that she understood how I felt and that she wished that she could take away my pain. Now, all of a sudden, instead of holding my hand, she was giving me a kick in the pants!

But, you know, that was exactly what I needed. The next day I went to school with a whole new attitude. I knew that it would be difficult to make friends after sulking for five months but I knew that I had to try.

I did try. I joined the band, went to the track meets, was friendly to all my classmates and excelled in my studies. Exactly one year later I was elected student council president.

Teachers, we need to encourage students to make the best of difficult circumstances. Life sometimes hands you disappointments, problems or tragedies. We need to develop the inner resources in our students that will allow them to prevail when difficulties arise. The road of life is not always smooth. Help students to be flexible and adaptable and to see the possibilities for navigating the bumps.

Speaking

My career took a dramatic change of directions in 1971 when I was asked to make a presentation to a local school district about how to help children become better readers. What began as an opportunity to share my ideas with twenty-one teachers in one building became the start of another career. I have now spoken to thousands of teachers, parents, administrators, school board members, business people and other groups throughout the United States, Canada and Europe.

The following stories pertain to the people that I have encountered, the adventures that I have had and to the insights that they have given me.

*Those having torches
will pass them on
to others.*

Plato

Strangest Stage

Teachers must be flexible and able to adapt to different environments. That is what enables us to sit on bleachers for three hours of in-service, supervise 200 kids in the gym when the power goes off, cower with twenty-seven kids in a bathroom during a tornado warning and cram three first-grade classes into one room when the other two rooms are invaded by wasps. Teaching was great training for speaking in unusual venues when I was on the road.

I was invited to give an opening-day-of-school speech in a beautiful, restored opera house. Upon arriving, I was greeted by a distressed superintendent who said, "We've got a problem."

I asked what was wrong and he said, "There's a set on the stage and we can't close the curtain. The set will be very distracting."

Unfazed I said, "Not to worry. Once I start talking, the teachers won't pay any attention to the set."

"You haven't seen the set," he warned.

I walked into the auditorium and started laughing. There were red chintz curtains on the windows, a saloon bar complete with festoons, gaudy overstuffed furniture and bras, panties and garter belts hanging from the chandelier of the set for "The Best Little Whorehouse in Texas."

When I walked on stage to begin my speech, I couldn't resist opening with, "Well, I've spoken in many venues but I've never spoken in a whorehouse before."

The Loudest Speech

Teachers learn to roll with the punches. When the overhead projector light bulb burns out just as we are going to tell a transparency story, we have our felt boards ready. When the electricity goes off, we are prepared to tell ghost stories.

Speakers also learn to go with the flow. When speakers' venues are distracting, we make jokes. Then we deliver the most engaging speeches that we can.

I was once asked to speak at an educational sorority luncheon at the Pontiac Silverdome in Pontiac, Michigan. When the program chairperson called to invite me, I was surprised. I had been to the Silverdome for football games and trade shows but I did not know that they had seminar rooms. She explained that I would be speaking in a lovely room that overlooked the playing field.

When I drove into the parking lot surrounding the Silverdome, I was impressed by the large number of cars. I knew that there had to be activities occurring besides the one that I was attending because only seventy-five people were expected at our meeting.

I found the conference room. There were large windows overlooking the field.

We had lunch and then I began to speak. My back was to the field. The audience was facing the field and me. They could not see the field because they were too far away from the windows.

About ten minutes into the speech, I heard the loudspeaker from the field and then a thunderous noise that could best be described as a freight train going "rrrrrrhhhhhh, rrrrrrhhhhhh, rrrrrrhhhhhh."

The sorority members looked away from me and out the windows.

I turned and saw a huge billow of smoke.

Within seconds, we heard this "rrrrrrhhhhhh, rrrrrhhhhhh, rrrrrrhhhhhh" train sound again and there was another huge plume of smoke.

I walked over to the window and looked down to see a tractor pull in full force.

I was thinking, "Who was the bright light that scheduled a speech at the Silverdome at the same time that a tractor pull was going on?" When I saw the poor program chairperson, who was in a complete tizzy, I remained silent and tried to make the best of a bad situation.

"Perhaps, if we ask the members to turn their chairs around and we put you on the opposite wall, they won't be distracted by the smoke," the chairperson suggested. I thought that it was worth a try.

We moved the podium and switched the chairs.

There were about two minutes of calm before it began again.

At least the audience wasn't distracted by the plumes of smoke, but it didn't help my concentration any because now I was looking straight at big black clouds floating past the window!

We had about five more episodes of the "rrrrrrhhhhhh" sounds. Although the members could avoid seeing the smoke, they could not ignore hearing the noise.

I persevered valiantly. After all, I had taught eighth graders. I wasn't going to let a little thing like a tractor pull stop me!

Before long, the program chairperson intervened.

"I think we had better call it a day," she sighed.

I brought my remarks to a brief conclusion.

Several members stayed to watch the rest of the tractor pull.

I left with the realization that, if I could talk opposite a tractor pull, I could speak just about anywhere anytime.

It also gave me another story to add to my repertoire. When other speakers begin to talk about the difficult conditions under which they've had to speak, I can always say, "Let me tell you about the time that I spoke opposite a tractor pull at the Pontiac Silverdome."

The Shortest
Speech

I was invited to do a forty-five-minute closing luncheon speech for a conference in an
Eastern state.

I flew in, taxied to the conference site and
joined the head table for lunch.

The program chairperson was seated next to
me. He said, "When we are through eating, I will
thank some of the conference organizers and
make a few general announcements. Then we are
having a raffle. After the raffle, I will introduce
you. That will probably be around 12:45. You will
have forty-five minutes. Just make sure you are
done by 1:30 because our members have flights to

catch at the airport. We cannot go beyond 1:30 or they will miss their flights."

"No, problem," I assured him. "Speakers are used to working on deadlines and, as a college professor of long standing, I can hit forty-five minutes on the mark."

Lunch concluded. The chairperson made his announcements and then turned the meeting over to the raffle organizer at 12:35.

She was a dynamic, entertaining lady who had obviously put a great deal of thought and effort into her assignment. She got the audience whooping and hollering for each prize that was won. People are always excited to win something, but these folks were really wound up!

The raffle continued. I looked at my watch. It was 12:55.

I turned to the chairperson, "If I start right now, I only have thirty-five minutes. Do you still want me to stop at 1:30?"

"Oh, yes. You have to," he replied.

I usually need about ten minutes to develop a theme. I had four major themes prepared to deliver so I mentally reorganized my speech and dropped a theme to fit the shorter time frame.

The raffle continued.

At 1:05 I leaned over to the chairperson and said, "It's now 1:05. That only leaves 25 minutes. Are you sure you want me to stop at 1:30?"

"Yes, our members are depending on getting out of here at 1:30. The raffle is taking much longer than anticipated. I am sure it will be completed momentarily."

I reorganized my speech, dropped another theme and waited.

At 1:25 the raffle concluded.

The chairperson conceded, "You can keep them until 1:35."

He stood up and said, "In the interest of giving our speaker as much time as possible, I present to you, with no further introduction, Dr. Mary Bigler."

With that being said, I was "on."

I had flown from Michigan to the East coast to give a ten-minute speech!

Good teachers adapt. We do our best with the students, resources and time given us.

The Most Embarrassing Speech (but not for me)

Traveling on the road is draining and stressful. To make it more bearable, one needs to find ways to have a good laugh.

We had just departed from St. Louis headed for Detroit when I turned to the woman sitting next to me and began a conversation which started with me asking her where she was from.

We had visited for ten or fifteen minutes when I said, "I'll bet you're a teacher."

She looked uneasy and seemed a little flustered. "How would you know that?" she asked warily.

"I'm a teacher, too, and I can usually spot one a mile away. I'll bet I can even tell what grade you teach."

"No way," she replied.

"I'll say kindergarten."

"Close, but no cigar. First grade," she laughed.

We continued our visit and then she said, "You really caught me off guard when you asked if I was a teacher, because I called in sick today. I'm flying to see my brother who is sick and I'm feeling rather sheepish about it. I didn't have any personal business days left. So I told a little white lie. When you asked me if I was a teacher, I envisioned you might be from the school district. I guess it's the guilt, huh?"

"Probably," I mused.

Realizing that first grade teachers are especially interested in reading, I asked, "Do you ever go to your state reading association convention?" Earlier in the conversation I had learned which state she was from so I knew that I was going to be doing the opening keynote for her convention in ten months.

"Oh, yes. The other first grade teacher and I try to go every year."

I was just about ready to say that I was going to be speaking there when she continued, "We usually just drive in early on the first day so we don't have to pay for a hotel room, but we're going early this year because there is supposed to be a really good opening keynote speaker the night before. We had to pay $75.00 for the hotel for that night so she'd better be worth it."

At that point I didn't want to say, "Guess what? I'm the speaker!" so I played it cool and continued the conversation.

A plan began to formulate in my mind. As we touched down, I said, "I'd love to have your name. You never know. We're both teachers and our paths may cross again."

She retrieved her business card from her purse. I looked at it and said, "It was nice visiting with you, Marina. I hope we meet again."

I filed her business card away in my state conventions' file.

Ten months later, I addressed her state reading convention.

During my speech I said, "I wonder if Marina Winks, a first grade teacher, is here?"

There was a murmur in the left rear of the auditorium. People were pointing to a lady near them.

I asked, "Marina, would you stand up?"

Marina stood. She had no idea who I was.

"Now, I want you all to know what pressure is. What if you were on a plane and a seatmate identified herself as a teacher and told you that she was going to a convention and that the opening keynote speaker had better be good because she, the teacher, had to pay $75.00 for a hotel room just to get to hear that speaker? And you were the speaker? Is that pressure or what?"

I could see Marina struggling to figure out what I was talking about.

"And don't worry, Marina. No one in your district will know that you called in sick to go see your brother."

About that time, she started to laugh and say, "Oh, no! I can't believe it's you. Oh, no!"

The audience was laughing. Marina was such a great sport. Afterwards, we went for coffee. People came up to her all night telling her what a great sense of humor she had.

Look for opportunities to put laughter in your classrooms and in your lives. You'll have less stress, live longer, teach better and have a lot more fun if you do.

The Most Self-Promoting Speech

I received a phone call around seven o'clock on a Thursday evening from a conference chairperson in Chicago. His reading consultant, scheduled to do several sessions on Friday, had just notified him that she was stranded on an island off the coast of Washington because of a ferry strike (I kid you not) and would not be able to get to Chicago. The chairperson asked if there was any way that I could come to Chicago to fill in.

Wanting to help, I assured him that I would find a way to get there.

I caught the last flight to Chicago.

After checking in at the hotel, I approached the elevator with the bellman. There were three ladies standing there. I just knew that they were teachers from the conference.

The first thing I heard was, "She can't be any good or she would have been on the program in the first place."

I knew that they were talking about me.

One of them said, "It's like having a substitute teacher. They are never as good as the regular teacher."

"And she's from Ann Arbor. It will be some research professor from the University talking about stuff we don't understand or we can't use," said the second lady.

The third lady said, "Well, I'm not getting up for that."

She took her pen and scratched out the session in her program booklet.

I was standing there taking this all in. Then I did something that I had never done before. As Flip Wilson would say, "The Devil made me do it."

I said, "Are you talking about the reading speaker that's coming tomorrow?"

"Yes."

"Well, she's terrific," I gushed.

"You've heard her before?"

I nodded emphatically, "Yes, several times."

What will she talk about?" queried one of the ladies.

"I'm not sure but she's funny and informative," I raved. "You'll love her."

"What was her name again?"

"It's something like Bickler or Bidler or something," I said.

"Bigler. Mary Bigler," one of the ladies said. "That's what I wrote down."

By this time the elevator arrived and we all got on.

As the elevator ascended, I began to feel guilty. What if they came to the workshop tomorrow and saw me and then started trying to reconstruct what they had said to me and become anxious that they might have offended me? I certainly did not want that to happen.

When we reached my floor, the door opened

and the bellman and I stepped out. I turned around and said, "By the way, my name's Mary Bigler."

I had just enough time to see their jaws drop before the doors closed.

As we walked toward the room, the bellman asked, "Were they talking about you? That's rude."

"Oh, it wasn't anything personal. They don't know me. They were just saying what anyone would say under the circumstances," I explained. I was touched because the bellman seemed genuinely concerned that my feelings might be hurt.

The next morning, I walked into the room where I was going to speak. There, sitting in the middle of the first row, were the three ladies from the elevator.

"Talked you into coming, huh?" I teased.

"We couldn't resist," they countered.

Seven years later, I took a shuttle bus at the airport in Orlando, Florida. I started visiting with the lady who sat next to me. It turns out that she was from Vancouver, British Columbia, and that we were both headed to the International Reading Association Convention.

I said, "I'd like to introduce myself. I'm Mary Bigler from Ann Arbor, Michigan."

"I know who you are," she chuckled. "In fact, the first time I met you, you told me what a terrific speaker you were."

"Chicago, Illinois," I laughed.

"Yup!" and she started telling the people in front of us the story.

The Most
Difficult Speech

I have had many adventures as a speaker. A
good number were amazing and inspiring. A
few were filled with trials and tribulations.
There is no question in my mind that the most
difficult speech that I ever gave was a back-to-
school speech in the mid 1980's.

The superintendent of a district had con-
tracted me to present a one-hour speech to
welcome the staff back for another school year.
About a month before the speech he called to say
that their contract negotiations were not going
well but he was certain that they would get everything settled before the first day. He called back a

167

week before the speech and said that they were still negotiating.

I said that I could not cross a picket line. He was sympathetic to that.

The night before I was to speak he called to say that they were still negotiating but he anticipated that they would settle the contract before 8:00 a.m. the following morning at which time I was scheduled to speak.

I suggested that, perhaps, I should come at a later date but he insisted that the scheduled opening would be held the next day.

I arrived at 7:30 a.m.

The teachers were picketing.

I sat in my car and thought that I would stay until 8:00 a.m. If the teachers were still picketing, I would return home.

About 7:45 a.m. someone came out of the building and talked to the teachers. The teachers put their picket signs down and entered the building.

I assumed that the strike had ended and I went into the building.

Clearly in a bad mood, the teachers were huddled together in small groups talking.

I went into the gym and found the superintendent on stage. I asked if he was sure that he wanted me to speak since the atmosphere in the building did not seem conducive to a back-to-school-rah-rah speech.

He said that he wanted me to do the speech.

The school board president, the superintendent and I took seats on the stage.

The superintendent arose to introduce the board of education president who was to welcome the teachers back for a new year.

When the superintendent stood up, the entire group of teachers stood up, as if on signal, turned their chairs around and faced the back of the gym.

The superintendent proceeded to deliver his introduction—to the backs of the teachers!

When the board president began his remarks, the superintendent sat down next to me. I leaned over and said, "I really don't think that the teach-ers are in any mood to listen to my remarks. Why don't I come back later in the year when things have settled down?"

The superintendent was firm, "The teachers are under a contractual obligation to be here today and they are going to listen to the opening-of-school speech."

Hoping to change his mind, I replied, "It really seems rather counter-productive."

The board president concluded his remarks to the backs of the teachers. The superintendent stood up to welcome the new teachers and to in-troduce me.

As the board president sat down, I pleaded my case, "I don't think that the teachers are going to get much out of my speech. They seem pretty upset. I would rather give this speech at a later date."

"They are not mad at you. They are upset with us. I am sure that they will turn their chairs around when you begin," he stated.

"Perhaps, but I don't think that they are going to be receptive to my message," I argued.

The superintendent concluded his introduction.

I stood up, to no applause, and whispered to the superintendent, "I don't think this is a good idea."

He said, "You have a contract. You are going to give the speech."

I truly thought that the teachers would turn their chairs around to face me when I began, but they did not.

I began my speech. I spoke for about two minutes and then looked helplessly at the superintendent as if to say, "Do you really want me to continue?"

He motioned for me to keep going.

I went on with the speech.

The next forty-five minutes seemed like forty-five days. For me to feel good about what I am doing, I need to know that my message is being received. On this day, I could barely tell that my audience was alive. Occasionally, I saw some shoulders moving with laughter or heard a few chuckles but that was it. This was the most demoralizing experience of my speaking life.

I concluded my speech, turned and left the stage without thanking the superintendent for inviting me and headed for my car.

Several teachers approached me and apologized, "We hope you understand that this had nothing to do with you. We're sorry, but we had to protest what's been going on and this was one way we could do it."

I replied, "I understand that you were angry and that you felt that you had to protest in some way, but I wouldn't have done what you did to a fellow teacher. If you want to show your administrators that you feel that they have treated you unfairly, that's one thing. But to be rude to a fellow teacher who is an invited guest to your district is another matter. I am sorry that you felt that you had to do that."

Although I was distressed by the combination of circumstances that caused this event to happen, I felt a sense of accomplishment that I completed the task that I had agreed to do under very trying circumstances. It has also given me a great story to share with fellow speakers. Whenever anyone tells a horror story about some speaking engagement, I say, "Let me tell you about the time that I spoke to the backs of my audience."

The Most
Frustrating Speech

We need to be courageous to be good teachers. We should always *work* for what is best for children. There are times when we have to *fight* for them as well.

I have done hundreds of in-services since 1971. I have only been asked to leave a school once before the in-service was scheduled to be concluded.

A middle school principal called to ask if I would be willing to come to his district to do a half-day in-service on reading instruction for the elementary school staff.

I asked what he wanted me to present and he

said, "I've heard you speak several times and your message on balanced literacy is just what the teachers need."

I did make note that it was the middle school principal inviting me to the elementary building, but I assumed that he was in charge of in-service for the district and gave it no more thought.

Planning to speak from 9:00 a.m. until noon, I arrived at the elementary school on the appointed day.

I spoke for an hour and a half and then took a break.

During the break, a gentleman approached me with a frown, "I am the principal of this building and I am very unhappy with your message. I want you to take back what you said."

I realized that he was much too serious to be kidding, "Take back what message?"

He answered, "The part about the importance of reading out loud to children. I do not believe in reading out loud to children. That is just what teachers do when they don't have anything else planned. It has no value. The *children* should be reading—not the teachers."

I was dumbfounded. Could any educator really believe this?

"I certainly agree that children need to be reading but I also believe that there is great value in teachers reading to children. Children have better listening vocabularies than reading vocabularies so teachers can read more complex material to them than children can read on their own. Teachers can introduce higher quality literature to children than they might select by themselves. Also, teachers are likely to read a variety of genres that children might not choose on their own." I continued with several other reasons supporting the value of teachers reading to children.

He persisted, "You and I do not agree on that and you are undermining my authority with my staff. I have told them not to read to children and, then, you come in here and say that they should. I want you to retract that."

"Sir, how can I do that? You want me to stand

up and say, 'Just forget everything that I have said in the last hour and a half. It's not true.' I would have no credibility if I did that. Besides, I don't believe that. It is important for teachers to read to children."

"You must take back what you said," he ordered. "I have reprimanded two of my teachers for reading aloud to students and they continue to defy me about that. Now you come in here and say that what they are doing is good. I repeat. You are undermining my authority."

"Reasonable people can differ, Mr. Principal. That's why we have jury trials. You are the boss in this building. You can tell your teachers to do whatever you think is best for children but I would be less than honest if I told you that you were right about this."

"You either take back what you said or I must insist that you leave," he commanded.

I was shocked.

"What?" I asked.

"You heard me," he said. "I can not support

people coming in here and saying the opposite of what I have told the staff. You must leave."

I was aghast but knew that he meant what he said. I packed up my material and headed out the door.

The teachers were coming back from the break. They said, "Where are you going? You are supposed to speak until noon, aren't you?"

"I have to leave," I replied and gave no further explanation.

By the time I got home, a very apologetic middle school principal had left a message to call him as soon as I got in.

I called and he apologized, "We are so embarrassed, Dr. Bigler. We should have been more forthright with you. You see, the elementary principal really is uninformed, highly opinionated and has a year to go until retirement. We know that he rules his building with an iron fist and that he just hasn't kept up on the latest research regarding reading instruction. The Superintendent has had so many complaints from the elementary staff about him. We thought, if someone could come in and validate what the teachers were doing, we could just work around him. We never dreamed he would do anything like this. We are so sorry."

"Don't feel sorry for me," I said. "Feel sorry for those teachers who have to work with him on a daily basis. Education is too important to leave to people who are 'uninformed' and that we have to 'work around'."

Many decisions in schools are made for the convenience of teachers, for the ease of administrators, for what is cheapest or for what is best for the bus schedule. Many decisions are made by people who are not as knowledgeable as they should be. Informed and courageous teachers need to understand what is best practice and then fight to deliver it.

My Sister and I Hate Mary Bigler

It is usually a good thing when my reputation as a speaker precedes me, but *there are exceptions.*

 I had flown to New York City to address a group of principals.

I was waiting in line at a taxicab stand at La-Guardia Airport when I began visiting with a young man standing in line behind me. He informed me that he was a college student from Wisconsin who was coming to the Big Apple for a summer internship and that he would be living with five other interns in an apartment. He knew no one in New York and had not been to the city before. He expressed apprehension about the situation.

I tried to encourage him with suggestions of all the interesting things that he could do while having an extraordinary opportunity to network for future job possibilities. I eventually explained that I had a daughter who had lived in the city for several years and that she would be a good resource if he needed to know where to get cheap groceries, what bank to use or what pharmacy or dry cleaners would be accessible to his neighborhood.

So I took out a sheet of paper and wrote down my daughter's email address. Then I put my name down so, if he wrote to my daughter, she would know how he had gotten her email. I handed the slip of paper to him.

With an incredulous voice he asked, "Mary Bigler! Are you a teacher?"

Somewhat surprised, I replied that I was.

"Do you speak at early childhood conferences in Wisconsin?"

"Well, yes, I have."

"At Whitewater, Wisconsin?" he pursued.

"I plead guilty."

"Oh, no! My sister and I hate you!"

"What did I ever do to you?" I asked in dismay.

"My mom is a preschool teacher and every year she would go to that early childhood conference and she would come home and say, 'Mary Bigler says you should read this. Mary Bigler says you should read that. Mary Bigler says our family should be doing this. Mary Bigler says our family should be doing that.' My sister and I had to write in a family journal, go to story hour at the library and only watch one hour of television a night because of you. We hated you. We dreaded our mother going to that conference every year because we knew that, when she came home, we'd have to listen to 'Mary Bigler says . . .'"

I laughed aloud while he continued, "My mother is never going to believe I met you. Would you write her a note?"

"Gladly." I took out a pen. "What's her name?"

He informed me that his mother's name was Pat so I wrote:

> *Dear Pat,*
>
> *You have a delightful son. We've gotten acquainted in a taxi line in New York City. You've done a good job. He's a nice young man—even if he does hate Mary Bigler.*
>
> *Warmly,*
> *Mary Bigler*
>
> *P.S. Thanks for implementing what you heard at the conferences. If more parents and teachers did that, we would have a lot more children succeeding in school.*

Bob Tomsich

I have had the privilege of working with many knowledgeable, intelligent, talented and inspiring educators. One of the most creative, effective and entertaining speakers that I have ever worked with is Bob Tomsich of Colorado. He has a tremendous sense of humor and loves practical jokes. He has one of those dog leashes with an imaginary dog on the end of it. He walks up to perfect strangers in the airport and asks them to hold the leash while he goes to the restroom. Some people actually stand there holding an imaginary dog!

Bob and I were scheduled to speak at a conference in Chicago. We both spoke during the first workshop session and then had an hour off before we had to speak again.

Bob suggested that we go into the hotel café for a Coke. The waitress brought the Cokes and we proceeded to drink them.

About the time we were finished, the waitress came to the table, looked at our empty glasses and gasped, "You drank the Cokes? Oh, no! I'm really going to be in trouble."

Then she left.

Bob and I looked at each other and he said, "What was that about?"

"I have no idea," I shrugged.

We were speculating about what was happening when the manager appeared with the waitress and said, "Now, folks, there's nothing to worry about. We're having a water problem here and the Health Department has said we can't serve any water because it has been chemically contaminated. This young lady just came on the floor and was not informed of this so she served you the fountain Cokes. But, don't worry because I have checked with the Health Department and they assure me that there's no danger at all. You shouldn't have any side effects. The worst thing—and it's unlikely—is you might have a little stomach upset which could cause a bout of diarrhea."

My first thought was that this was one of Bob's practical jokes. So I said accusingly, "Bob, this isn't funny."

"What are you talking about, Mary? I didn't do this."

"Bob, I'm not kidding. Chemical contamination scares me."

The manager said, "Ma'am, I assure you. This is not serious. I just wanted you to know why the waitress said what she did."

The waitress and manager left and I said, "Bob, they are serious."

"I know," he replied. "What I don't need is a diarrhea attack in the middle of my speech."

I laughed in spite of myself.

We left the café and went to do our speeches. About half way through the workshop, Bob came running through my room, up and down the aisle, waving two fingers in the air, which, of course, is the universal school symbol for having to go to the restroom for a bowel movement.

I started laughing and had to tell the audience about what had happened in the café. We all had a good laugh.

Incidentally, Bob did not have a diarrhea attack. He was just trying to shake me up by making me think that I was next.

Whenever I am giving a speech in a hotel room and the door opens, I half expect to see Bob coming down the aisle with two fingers in the air.

Nancy Johnson

Nancy Johnson is a dynamic consultant in gifted education from southern Illinois. She and I worked many of the same conferences for a good number of years. We look a great deal alike, have similar speaking styles, use a lot of humor and are practical in our approach to educational issues. Nancy tells the following story.

She was in the Philadelphia airport and was "tackled from behind" by a lady who said, "Oh, my gosh. It's you! I have heard you speak several times. You are wonderful! I've used so many of your ideas. I did the teacher want ad. I patterned *Brown Bear, Brown Bear.* I had my students do fact/response cards. My second graders just love all your ideas. I just can't believe I'm actually getting to talk to you!"

Nancy was puzzled because she had no idea what the lady was talking about. The activities that the lady described were not familiar to her. Nancy did not quite know how to respond but, ever gracious, she said, "I'm so glad they are helpful to you."

"Oh, they are. I've shared them with lots of the teachers in my building. The fifth grade teacher said the transcription of song lyrics really encouraged some of her reluctant writers to put pen to paper."

"That's great," replied the perplexed Nancy. "We can use all the help that we can get to engage those reluctant writers. I wish that I had more time so we could visit, but I have a plane to catch."

"Of course," replied the lady. "It was delightful talking to you. I just can't wait to get back to my school to tell the other teachers that I got to talk to Mary Bigler in the Philadelphia airport!"

Nancy said that she did not have the heart to tell the lady that she had us mixed up. The teacher had obviously seen both of us speak and had us confused. I told Nancy that she should have said, "Well, if you like my ideas so much, you really need to hear Nancy Johnson. She's even better!"

Jessica's Mom

I always tell parents to read to their children from the time that they get them until the time that their children leave. Parents need to know that they can read more complicated material to children than the children can read on their own. They can introduce more difficult vocabulary, more complex sentence structures and more abstract ideas than children could read on their own. Opportunities are presented to discuss sensitive topics as they arise in a story. Without such an occasion, such conversations are sometimes neglected. As we have seen with Lateesha's family, the bonding that occurs when parents read to their children is priceless. Let me tell you about a parent who reminded me of this valuable lesson.

I gave a PTA speech one night and I said, "Read to your children from the time that you get them until the time that they leave you. If they are still living with you at age thirty, kick them out, but read to them while they are leaving."

Three years later I went back to the same school and gave a similar speech.

Afterwards a lady came up to me and said, "I'm so disappointed."

I frowned, "About what?"

"You said something when I heard you three years ago that you did not say tonight."

"What was that?"

"When I heard you three years ago, you said, 'Read to your children from the time that you get them until the time that they leave you.' You didn't say that tonight. I think you should have."

"You're right," I replied. "I should have said that. I almost always say that. I believe that. I just forgot to say it tonight."

"I'm telling you that statement revolutionized my life. Let me tell you what happened after I heard you speak three years ago. My daughter, Jessica, was fifteen years old. I hadn't read to her in at least five years. I didn't know that I should keep reading to her. I figured, once she was able to read on her own, she didn't need me any more so I quit reading to her."

"When I heard you, you made it sound so important that I read to her that I went home and told my daughter, "I heard this speaker tonight. She said I should read to you. So, from now on, we are going to read together every night for fifteen or twenty minutes. You can pick something out or I'll select something, but we are going to read every night.' "

Jessica rolled her eyes and said, "Mom, that's dumb. I'm fifteen years old!"

Mom informed her that this wasn't negotiable and that she didn't need any attitude from her.

Jessica said, "Don't go to any more meetings up at the school."

The first night, Mom said, "We're going to read now. Do you want to pick something out?"

In the tone of voice that only an exasperated fifteen-year-old can muster, she said, "No!"

Mom said, "Okay. Well, let's read something from the *Reader's Digest*."

Jessica counted the ceiling tiles.

The next night Mom said, "We're going to read now. Do you want to pick something out?"

Jessica snarled, "You don't need to ask me, Mom. I'm not going to pick anything out."

"OK," Mom replied. "Let's read something from *Seventeen*."

Jessica glared at her.

Sticking to her guns, Mom repeated the request again the next night.

"Mom, I told you, I'm not picking anything out to read."

"Okay. Let's read something from *Guideposts*."

I guess that did it because, the next night, Jessica threw something on the coffee table when it was time to read. They started reading Steinbeck's, *The Pearl*, a school assignment.

That was the beginning.

Mom said that they had been reading together for the last three years. She said that it was the very best time that they had together. They had begun recommending books to each other. They had bought books as gifts for friends and relatives. They had shared many discussions about values and attitudes because of their reactions to the stories and articles that they had read together.

Then she said, "Dr. Bigler, this fall, Jessica left to go away to college. She called me in November to let me know that she was making her first visit home. She said, 'Mom, I'm coming home Friday. Get a book ready.' "

"Dr. Bigler, you must keep telling parents to read to their children. I never would have known to do it and it has been the best thing that's happened for my relationship with Jessica."

Parents, you are your children's first and most important teacher. So read to your children from the time that you get them until

the time that they leave you. It is the best thing that you can do to build the foundation for their success in school and to develop your relationship with them.

Love You Forever

I never hold Love You Forever *in my hand without thinking of a very courageous woman and
the daughter that she will love forever.*

I presented a program at a PTA meeting entitled, "Raising Readers." I talked about the
value of reading to children, encouraged parents
to read to their children and shared some of my
favorite books. Among those books was a beautiful
story by the Canadian storyteller and author
Robert Munsch. He wrote a heart-warming story
entitled, *Love You Forever.*

Although it is a children's book, I find, like
most good books, that there are messages for
everyone. I think that adults relate to this book as

much as children do but for different reasons. The story is about a mother who has a new baby boy. She sings and rocks the baby and tells him that he will always be her baby and that she will love him forever. The story follows the baby into adulthood where the roles eventually become reversed and the man is rocking his mother and telling her that he will love her forever. Kids sometimes think this part is funny but, for those of us who have lived long enough, the ending is truer to life than we might like it to be.

This particular night I read excerpts from that story.

At the conclusion of the program, a mother approached me.

She had tears in her eyes as she said, "Thank you for sharing *Love you Forever.* It is such a wonderful story. It has special significance for me. You see, I buried my six-year-old daughter three weeks ago. She had meningitis. *Love You Forever* was her favorite book and we read it every night before bedtime. I placed it in her coffin."

I felt numb all over my body and could not think of anything to say.

"Please keep telling parents to read to their children," she continued. "We are all so busy. It is hard to find the time to do it, but none of us knows how long we will have the opportunity. I feel good that I read as much as I did to my daughter. We shared so much together through stories."

"I am so sorry for your loss," I meekly offered.

"You will probably think this is crazy but I went out and bought a new copy of *Love You Forever*. I still read it to her every night."

"I don't think that's crazy at all," I said through my tears.

"Just keep spreading the message," she implored.

As she walked away, I was struck by the fact that a children's picture book had contributed so much to the way this caring mother had interacted with her daughter. By continuing to read the book aloud each night, she had found a way to stay connected to her beloved daughter and to make the worst of pains more bearable.

What a remarkable lady! Even in her grief she was able to reach out to me to thank me and to encourage me to keep reminding parents of the bond that they can forge when they read to their children. May her story help us all to "just keep spreading the message."

Velma

Psychologist Karl Menninger said, "What the teacher is, is more important than what he teaches." We do not remember the philosophies or strategies of teachers. We remember the teachers. I have been inspired and humbled by hundreds of extraordinary teachers that I have met around the world. Let me introduce you to one.

It was worth the long trip to south Texas to meet Velma. The eighth of twelve children of migrant parents, she was a teacher in a Texas border town. She invited me to come to her school to work with her colleagues. In the brief time that we had when she drove me from the airport to the hotel, she told me this story.

Velma's family worked as pickers in the fields. The fourteen of them lived in a two-room shack with dirt floors. Her parents had never gone to school and had never learned to read and write. Her dad dreamed that one of his children would graduate from high school.

When Velma finished eighth grade, she told her father that she was dropping out of school as all of her siblings had done before her.

Her father said that he thought that she was the one child that he had who might be able to graduate from high school. He asked her to take a sheet of paper and make a contract. He told her to write, "I will be a good girl and stay in school." He asked her to sign it and he signed with an "X." He told her that, if she was a good girl and stayed in school, he would not ask her to pick in the fields anymore.

In the fall, Velma started high school.

After the first week, Velma's dad asked her if there was anything that she needed for school.

She told him that there was nothing that she

needed but there was something that she wanted. She wanted to play in the school band. The band director had said that they needed a clarinet player, so Velma wanted a clarinet.

Several weeks later her father appeared with a clarinet. He had done some welding work for a rancher and was paid with a clarinet.

Velma started practicing and became very good in a short amount of time. By the time that she graduated from high school, she qualified for a music scholarship at a junior college two hundred miles from her home.

While completing two years at the junior college, she lived with a family for whom she cooked and cleaned. She then transferred to a university where she qualified for a minority women's scholarship. She became a teacher and returned to her hometown to teach.

I asked her why she came back to her hometown when she could have had her choice of jobs anywhere in the country.

For her the answer was simple, "If I don't work with my people, who will?"

Velma serves as an important role model for poor, young people. In her purse Velma still carries the now tattered contract that she made with her dad. She tells her students that dreams, hard work and persistence enable you to do what you want in life.

Velma's wise and caring father not only had a child who finished high school and college. He had a child who has made a difference in the lives of hundreds of children because she is a teacher.

Big Old Gus

This is not my story but it is a great story about what it means to be a teacher. Leland Jacobs was a beloved education professor and educational speaker who spent most of his career at Columbia Teacher's College in New York City. He began his teaching career in a one-room schoolhouse in the Lincoln School District in southeast Michigan at the age of nineteen. This is his story.

Jac (pronounced Jake) had a student that he affectionately called "Big Old Gus." Gus was not a distinguished scholar but was loved by his classmates for his simple, affectionate nature.

Spiritual leader Mahatma Ghandi said, "The best textbook for a pupil is his teacher." There is no doubt that Jac was a most important textbook for Gus.

Jac loved poetry and recited poems whenever he could. When Jac would ask his class what poems they wanted him to recite, Gus would always ask for a poem by T. A. Daly entitled "Between Two Loves." Jac said that he must have recited it one hundred times in the year that he taught Gus.

Jac left that school after a year and began teaching at Michigan State Normal College (now Eastern Michigan University). One day, an English professor called Jac and said that a local school district was having a speech contest. The school had selected the top speaker in each class but they wanted an impartial committee of college teachers to select the school-wide winner. The English professor asked Jac if he would be interested in being a judge.

Jac agreed and asked what district was having the contest.

The professor replied that it was Lincoln.

Jac was delighted and said, "I used to teach in Lincoln. Maybe I'll know some of the kids."

On the appointed day and time, the professors walked into the gym and saw the finalists sitting up on the stage. Jac could hardly believe his eyes when he realized that one of the finalists was Big Old Gus.

One by one, the students gave their recitations.

When Gus stood up, he said, "I am reciting a poem by T.A. Daly. It is called 'Between Two Loves'."

Jac said it was like hearing a recording of himself reciting that poem. Every nuance, every pause, every inflection was Jac's.

When the last speaker had finished, the judges had to vote. Jac said that he did not know whom the other judges favored, but there was no doubt in his mind who was getting *his* vote.

When the votes were tallied, Big Old Gus was named the school-wide winner. It was the first and only academic award that he ever received.

Jac worked his way through the crowd and up onto the stage. He patted Gus on the back and said, "Gus, I'm so proud of you. You recited the poem perfectly. You must have read that poem a thousand times to recite it that well."

Big Old Gus chuckled, "Don't be silly, Mr. Jacobs. I've never read it."

Howard

The Roman writer Persius said, "He who en-
dures conquers." Howard not only endured
but proved, once again, that it is never too
late to learn.

I gave a presentation to parents in a poor,
southeast Michigan school district. After the
speech, a lady approached me and said, "See that
man, back there?"

I looked over her shoulder in the direction in
which she was pointing with her head and saw
this large, angry-looking man, arms folded, sitting
in the last seat in the auditorium.

In a rush of words she explained, "That's my fiancée. His name is Howard. We had a terrible

fight about coming here tonight. He's so mad at me and I don't even know why. He wouldn't even sit with me. See how he's sitting in the back and I was up front? He's really mad and I don't even know what I did. I don't think he's even going home with me. I told him there was a reading meeting up at the school that we had to go to. He said he wasn't going and I said he was and he said he wasn't. I told him the teachers said that parents have to be involved with their children's schooling and that he was going to be the father of my children so we had to come to this meeting. Well, he's here but he's really upset. Will you go talk to him?"

Not wanting to get involved in their argument, I said, "Ma'am, I don't think it would be wise for me to talk to him. I really wouldn't know what to say."

She said, "Oh, please. He's so angry. Just say something to calm him down."

Not wanting to approach the man, I said, "You know, I think it might make matters worse for a perfect stranger to try to talk to him."

She begged, "I don't know what to do."

The lady was desperate and I just couldn't refuse her. With great trepidation I started walking to the back of the auditorium. I had no idea what I was going to say but, just before I reached him, I think the Man Upstairs took pity on me and gave me the right words to say.

I walked up to him and said, "Your fiancée tells me that you didn't want to come here tonight. You know, it takes a pretty big man to walk into a school when school must have been a pretty tough place for him."

With that, the man broke down sobbing. Now I'm not talking a couple of tears inching down his face. I mean he broke down. I wouldn't have been more surprised if he had hauled off and hit me.

I was floored. People were looking at us and I'm thinking, "Good heavens! They must wonder what I said to him."

"School was rough, huh?" I said.

I wish I would have had a video camera to record his first words to me because I would show the tape to every teacher in the country. He looked up through his tears and said, "I thought you were going to ask me to read something out loud."

You see, his fiancée had said that he had to go to "a reading meeting" at the school. All of the embarrassment and frustration that he had experienced years ago trying to learn to read had come flooding back. He had dug in his heels and had resisted going back to school for fear of being humiliated yet again.

"Reading was hard for you?" I asked.

Pointing to his fiancée, he whispered, "I can't read, but she doesn't know it."

I said, "Let me tell you something. You ought to level with her. She loves you and wants you to be the father of her children. She might even be able to help you learn to read."

"No," he insisted. "I don't want her to know."

"That's your call, but I think you should be honest with her. She cares about you."

"No. I don't want her to know I'm stupid."

"You're not stupid," I assured him. "There

could be a lot of reasons why you didn't learn to read when you were in school that have nothing at all to do with intelligence. You could have been sick a lot and missed important instruction when you were a kid. Maybe you moved a lot. Maybe the methods and materials that the teachers used were not appropriate for you. Maybe you had a learning disability and, back when you were in school, the teachers might not have known what to do to help you."

He shook his head, "No. I'm stupid. The teachers told me I was."

I paused wanting to say just the right thing, "I want to apologize for any teacher who ever told you that you were stupid. Sometimes teachers get frustrated and say things that they don't mean. Have you ever done that? Well, some teacher probably tried to teach you to read and got aggravated because she wasn't successful and said that out of frustration, but I don't believe for one minute that you're stupid."

"Yes, I am. If you can't read, you're stupid. Everybody knows that."

"*I* don't know that. And, as long as we are visiting here like this, I don't want to hear you call yourself that." Then I asked, "Would you like to learn to read?"

"Well, sure. Who wouldn't want to know how to read?"

"What would you like to be able to read?" I asked.

He thought for a moment, "You won't laugh?"

"No, I won't laugh," I promised.

"I'd like to be able to read the *TV Guide*."

"There's nothing wrong with that."

"Do you know why?"

"I suppose it's because you want to know what's on at a particular time so you can watch your favorite programs."

"No," he said. "It's because of her kids. You see, they come up to me with the *TV Guide* and say, 'Howard, what's on at 7:30?' And do you know what I do? I push them away and say, 'Don't bother me. I'm tired. Go ask your mother.' I know it's wrong when I'm doing it. I'm being a mean SOB. It's not right. Those kids are nice kids and I'm yelling at them because I don't want them to know I can't read. You know what? My Old Man did the same thing to me. I bet he couldn't read either but we never knew it."

I smiled, "Howard, I've never heard a better reason to learn to read. Let me tell you what we are going to do. I know a lot of people who love to tutor adults in reading. They wouldn't charge you anything. If you agree to meet with them for a couple of hours a week at the local library, they will be thrilled to teach you. You give me a phone number where you can be reached and I'll set it up for you."

He cautioned, "Don't call me at her house."

"I'll call you at whatever number you give me. Do you have a job?"

"Yeah," he said.

"Okay. Give me your work number."

"But don't tell her," he said pointing to his fi-ancée again.

"Howard, I won't tell her but I really think that you should."

I left that school, returned home, made several phone calls the next day, got Howard a tutor and checked several months later to see if he was at-tending his lessons.

He was. The tutor reported that he was making slow, but steady progress.

That was my last communication about Howard.

Two years later I returned to the same school to make a similar speech. On the way there, I started thinking about Howard and his fiancée and wondering if they might be there that night.

I walked into the auditorium and the first peo-ple I saw were Howard and his fiancée. She came right up to me displaying her left hand proudly proclaiming, "We're married! We're married!"

"How, wonderful. I am so happy for you," I

said. Of course, I wasn't going to mention anything about Howard's reading.

Howard spoke right up, "I've got a present for you."

"You don't have to give me a present."

"Oh, yes I do. But I need your phone number. It's going to be delivered to you tonight. Will you be home by eleven?"

I thought it was peculiar, but I gave him my phone number. On the way home I was thinking about what the present might be. I thought, "A pizza!" (That's just how my mind works.)

The phone rang around 11:15. Howard's voice, bursting with pride, came through the line, "Dr. Bigler?"

"Yes."

"7:30, Channel 4, Seinfeld . . . " Howard proceeded to read the entire *TV Guide* entry. THAT was my present. In two years, Howard had learned to read well enough to read the *TV Guide*! It was the best present that I had ever received.

Lessons Learned

Teachers are ordinary people called to do an extraordinary job. Yet, many people do not appreciate this demanding career. We have all heard people say, "Those who can do. Those who can't teach" or "What a soft job teachers have. They have the whole summer off!" I never met a good teacher who had the summer off. We have summers to read journals, go to workshops, take courses, write curricula, plan new units, select textbooks, make bulletin boards, schedule field trips and guest speakers for the next school year, etc., etc., etc. We are always thinking about teaching. How can I use this in my class? Where can I get thirty pumpkins to carve? Can I find a canoe for my Lewis and Clark unit?

Teaching is not a vocation for the faint of heart. It is society's most important and challenging profession. At no time in our history have there been more demands and expectations placed upon us. Students must perform well on tests so policy makers can assure the public that we are turning out a good product. We are asked to produce responsible, skilled, productive citizens who are life-long learners. They must be trustworthy individuals who respect themselves and others. They need to be able to think independently and, yet, be team players. They have to be technologically literate to compete in an information age and a global world. They should enjoy the quest for knowledge and be able to find their passion and joy. They ought to understand the world and their place in it.

As teachers, our attention should be focused on creating the best possible learning environment so that our students can acquire those skills and attitudes. To do that, we must know what effective instruction is and must understand the research that drives that instruction. We must continually evolve in the art and craft of teaching. We must keep learning so that we can keep teaching effectively. Let's see what we have learned from my family, students, teachers, colleagues, and audiences that might help us to meet the challenges of our calling.

"Miss Boddicker" shows us that life lessons are more important than class lessons. Take the time to teach them. If you want to show your students that they can overcome obstacles, model this in yourself. Convey that anything is possible. Bury "can't" under Joe G. Boddicker's tree.

"Tom" underscores that we must teach our students to overcome obstacles. We must teach them to play to their strengths and accommodate their weaknesses. We must instill in our students the belief that they can succeed if they keep looking for a way and if they keep using the talents that they have.

"Grammar" encourages us to take risks. If we want our classrooms to come alive, we must come alive. If we want our students to know that it is good for them to takes risks, we have to take risks ourselves. We have to do whatever it takes to make learning relevant, exciting or just plain fun.

"Mr. R" demonstrates the importance of respecting our students. There is something special and unique in each of our students. They should be appreciated for their diversity and valued for what they bring to the classroom. We should use their personal experiences to enhance everyone's learning. We must help our students to find their gifts, to nurture them and to integrate them into their lives.

"Ross" reminds us that we should not always be two-by-four teachers, bound by the two covers of a book and the four walls of a classroom. At times, we must do more than stand in front of our students. Sometimes, we must stand shoulder to shoulder with them. On some occasions, we must stand up for them outside of class.

"Ross" also teaches us that our students need to know and like themselves in order to have the confidence that will enable them to make their way in the world. Let's help our students to be true to themselves as they make the decisions necessary to lead full and productive lives.

"Danny" helps us to remember that, while almost anyone can teach the skilled and motivated students, we earn our stripes on the hard-to-reach ones. We must show our get-around-the-rule kids how to use their ingenuity in more productive ways. We must help such minds to see that they can find greater challenges and delights in learning than in avoiding learning.

"Mike" prompts us to go beyond the ABC's. Our high-risk students will be feared tomorrow if we don't intervene on their behalf today to influence their attitudes, skills and behaviors. We must make the effort to form attitudes in our students that lead to qualities such as Mike developed: self-discipline and consideration.

"Darius and Jon" shows us that, although it may be good to *use* our tempers in our classrooms, it is never good to *lose* our tempers in our classrooms. As much as possible, we need to make "the punishment fit the crime." We must not produce negative learning in our attempt to create positive behavior. As much as possible, we should involve students in finding appropriate solutions which will move them toward the good conduct that we seek. On those few occasions when our frustrations get the best of us, we must find the character and the courage to admit our mistakes and to remedy them as soon as possible.

"Arlen" impresses upon us that capable and creative minds need to be channeled into life affirming thoughts. The young people in our classrooms are infinitely more important than the content that we are teaching them. They will be our future leaders, employers, neighbors, friends and in-laws. We leave an indelible mark upon each of them. As we instruct, guide, discipline and inspire them, we must be positive examples so that they become productive and responsible citizens who contribute their talents for the betterment of mankind.

"Lateesha," "Jessica" and "Love You Forever" all affirm that we must keep encouraging parents to be active in the education of their children. We need to remember that we do not just teach students. We teach families. Teachers become part of the families when the families become part of the school. In some cases, we might be the most educated people that parents encounter. They respect and trust us. We can help them be more effective parents by sharing our knowledge with them. Specifically, we must impress upon parents how important it is to continue reading to their children as long as they are home—not only for academic growth but also for the special connection and joy that can be shared by parent and child. As the courageous mother in "Love You Forever" said, "Just keep spreading the message."

As recounted in "Dad," my father passed on his legacy of honesty, fairness and responsibility to me and, through me, to my students. Now, it is being passed on to you. Teachers, we should be giving ourselves and our students wonderful legacies to emulate. As we strive to create skilled and knowledgeable students, let us not forget to produce honest, considerate, kind, caring and responsible citizens as well.

"Mom" illustrates that there are times when we need to be sympathetic, supportive, and encouraging, but there are also times when we need to be frank, demanding, and tough. Sometimes we need to put our feet down, draw lines in the sand, or deliver swift kicks. We need to prepare our students for the rough spots in life and to teach them how to triumph over adversity.

"The Shortest Speech," "The Loudest Speech," "The Strangest Stage," "Dog Pooh" and "The Filing Cabinet" all make the point that we need to expect the unexpected and that we need to be flexible and adaptable. We cannot always control what calamities befall us but we can control our responses to them.

The field trip stories show us that, even though we try to plan for every possibility, there will be times when fate works against us. We all make misjudgments, we all suffer from our limitations and we all have experiences in life which are not fair. When such things happen, we must do what we would want our students to do. We must pat ourselves on the back for waging the good fight, learn what we can from our failures and resolve to do better in the future.

"Senior Advisor" emphasizes the value of resourcefulness for a teacher. Whether it involves negotiating with local merchants to donate prizes for the holiday bizarre, enticing our colleagues into making our bulletin boards in exchange for doing their recess duty, or securing flowers for graduation, we always need to be vigilant to find ways to get what our students need. A well-known proverb is, "Where there's a will, there's a way." We need to say, "Where there's a teacher, there's a way!"

Before we condemn our colleagues for not being like us, let's remember "Margaret." We all have gifts to give children, but they are different gifts. We do not want all teachers to be the same. If we had a whole building full of Mary Biglers, all the kids would be ADHD. We need all of us with our different personalities, philosophies, methods and materials because we have a diversity of students with a variety of learning styles. Let's appreciate that one type of teacher is not the best for all students. Be grateful for the unique and diverse gifts that our fellow teachers bring to our students.

"Bill" brings home to us the power of praise and great expectations. If we want our students to be positive, then we must focus on the positive within them. If we look for the good in our students, we will find it. If we expect great things from our students, we will get them.

By all means, let's put laughter in our classrooms. The research shows that children learn most efficiently and effectively when they are relaxed and happy. Students do not learn well when they are afraid or tense. Whether it's through writing teacher want ads or through repartee and banter as in "Ross" or through a little teasing as in "The Most Self-Promoting Speech" or "The Most Embarrassing Speech" or via sight gags such as Bob Tomsich's two fingers in the air or his invisible dog, laughter in the classroom tells the students that this is a fun place to be. Our classrooms must be emotionally safe and pleasant places for learning.

Let's not let our political or other differences get in the way of supporting our colleagues as happened in "The Most Difficult Speech." We have few enough allies as it is. We should support each other whenever we can.

As informed and reflective teachers, we need to understand what makes the best learning environment for our students and, then, we must work to create it. But, sometimes, working is not enough. There are times when we can't back down—when we have to stand up and be counted. Perhaps that is why novelist Pearl Buck said, "Only the brave should teach." Let's draw courage from "The Most Frustrating Speech" to fight, in the face of ignorance and opposition, for what is best for our students.

Let's use "Nancy Johnson" to help us to be kind and gracious to those who make mistakes. Mistakes are the building blocks of success. We want our students and staffs to know that mistakes will happen but that errors pave the way for ultimate success. Educator Marva Collins said, "If you can't make a mistake, you can't make anything." We all have had students who did not have the self-confidence to make a guess. We must encourage them to try. We must reassure them that they don't have to be right. We must persuade them that they can attempt things in our classrooms without being penalized if they don't work out. I tell my students that they don't have to be perfect in my classroom but they have to try because the greatest mistake is to do nothing. As opera singer Beverly Sills so aptly said, "You may be disappointed if you fail, but you are doomed if you don't try." Our students need to understand that Babe Ruth achieved greatness because he hit 714 home runs, but he had to strike out 1,300 times to do it.

"Velma" reaffirms for us the tremendous influence that parents can have on a child's education even if the parents have little education themselves. When parents make their expectations and hopes clear to their children and do their best to encourage and support education, great things can happen. "Velma" shows how much can be accomplished by a student who comes from even the humblest of circumstances when she receives such parental support.

"Velma" also shows us a model of commitment that we all can admire. We don't teach for the money or the vacations. We don't keep struggling to rise above mounting administrative demands, declining budgets, accountability and testing pressures and the host of other problems that confront us because we think we have a cushy job. Remember Velma on those days when you leave your classroom discouraged and exhausted and ask, "I wonder if they are taking applications at Wal-Mart?" We're here for the same reason as Velma. We have an undying commitment to help our students and our communities to be the best that they can be. Take comfort that Velma and thousands of others like her are out there with us keeping the flame of education alive.

"Big Old Gus" and "Mr. K, The Math Principal,"

remind us that we aren't just teaching the curriculum. We are teaching ourselves. We are sharing our knowledge, our values, our character, our expectations, our joys and our passions. Students read us as surely as they read the books that we place in front of them. We teach who and what we are. That is all we can teach. That is why we must strive to be the best role models possible.

Theodore Roosevelt's maxim is so true: "No one cares how much you know until they know how much you care." When we share what we care about, it has an infectious effect on our students. Speaker and businessman Art Coombs said that the three things that his research could verify about what makes a good teacher were (1) good teachers communicate that they care about their students, (2) they care about what they're teaching and (3) they convey that what they're teaching is important to their students. We need to communicate what we care about to our students.

"Howard" proves that we must never allow our students to give up. It is never too late to learn. We need to cultivate persistence and resilience in the face of adversity. We must convince our students that, as long as they keep striving to succeed, they have within themselves the ability to triumph over the problems of life.

Afterthoughts

There will always be papers to grade, forms to complete, lesson plans to write, parents to call and meetings to attend but we must never forget the reasons why we committed to this calling. We're not here for the INCOME but for the OUTCOME. We're here to make a difference in the lives of others—to open the doors of the world to our students.

We're here to teach the facts and develop the skills that will be measured on the tests, but we're also here to teach what can't be measured on tests. We're here to impart what will only be evident in how our students live their lives. We're here to model and foster flexibility, resourcefulness, consideration, commitment, self-discipline, responsibility, honesty, courage, self-confidence, determination, respect, tolerance, grace, compassion, support, good humor, passion, and joy. We're here to remind others that all children don't learn at the same pace or in the same way. We're here to celebrate the unique heritage of each of our students as well as the diverse teaching styles of our colleagues. We're here to do whatever is necessary to make learning an exciting adventure in our classrooms. We're here to prepare our pupils to hurdle the barriers of life. We're here to be dream makers, not dream breakers. We're here to praise success and to encourage and honor the attempts to achieve it. We're here to find ability and goodness and to expect greatness and to enable our students to find those qualities within themselves. We're here to fight for the best interests of our students. We're here to impact our students, their parents and our colleagues so that the world is a better place for us having been in it.

Thank You, Reader

Thank you for allowing me to share these experiences and reflections with you. I hope that they enrich, fortify and inspire you as you pursue the crucial and exhilarating profession that you have chosen.

BOOK ORDERS

To order additional copies of *Mary Bigler's Lessons Learned* or to order any of Mary's current recommendations of pre-kindergarten through grade twelve books for students or her recommendations of resource and inspirational books for teachers, please visit the **Reading Success Center** website:

www.readingsuccesscenter.com

If you'd like to receive Mary's current recommendations and future updates, please email:

reading@ameritech.net

You may also contact the **Reading Success Center** via the following phone and fax numbers:

(877) 995-1053 (toll-free)
(734) 995-1053
(734) 995-2765 (FAX)